Instant Pot Multicooker Slow Cooker Cookbook

The Complete Multicooker Slow Cooker Guide with Delicious and Flavorful Recipes to Balance Your Meals

By Shawn B. White

Copyright ©2020 - By Shawn B. White

All Rights Reserved.

The content contained within this book may not be reproduced, duplicated or transmitted without direct written permission from the author or the publisher.

Under no circumstances will any blame or legal responsibility be held against the publisher, or author, for any damages, reparation, or monetary loss due to the information contained within this book, either directly or indirectly.

Legal Notice:

This book is copyright protected. It is only for personal use. You cannot amend, distribute, sell, use, quote or paraphrase any part, or the content within this book, without the consent of the author or publisher.

Disclaimer Notice:

Please note the information contained within this document is for educational and entertainment purposes only. All effort has been executed to present accurate, up to date, reliable, complete information. No warranties of any kind are declared or implied. Readers acknowledge that the author is not engaged in the rendering of legal, financial, medical or professional advice. The content within this book has been derived from various sources. Please consult a licensed professional before attempting any techniques outlined in this book.

By reading this document, the reader agrees that under no circumstances is the author responsible for any losses, direct or indirect, that are incurred as a result of the use of the information contained within this document, including, but not limited to, errors, omissions, or inaccuracies

CONTENT

Introduction

Are you tired of your kitchen being filled with many cooking appliances? Do you wish to own a kitchen appliance that will save you so much space? Do you wish to eat the most delicious and nicely cooked food? Instant Pot multicooker slow cooker is the kitchen appliance that you need.

Food has been and will always be among the most important things in the human life. Therefore, investing in the best cooking appliances for your kitchen should be your ultimate goal. Before I came know about the Instant Pot multicooker slow cooker, I always believed that it does not matter how you cook your food as long as you cook it.

Growing up in with my grandmother was perhaps among the best things in my life. She loved cooking so much that she would, every now and then, try out new recipes. It is from her that I developed my love for trying new recipes. She could surprise the family with delicious meals and constantly said that cooking nice and delicious foods is a great way of expressing love. Who does not want to be shown love? I guess no one.

Grandma owned a slow cooker which she used to prepare most of her meals. She loved it so much because the food cooked by the slow cooker was more delicious compared to that cooked otherwise. Beef and lamb were my favorites. If she had visitors coming to see her, she would always prepare them delicious meals using the slow cooker.

When I left for college, I was excited but then I was sad that I was going far away from grandma. Among the things I was definitely going to miss was her delicious food. Before I left, I vowed to take a keener look at how she prepared her meals so that I could learn more. I knew if I do not use the short time before I left, I would be left wishing that I did. For all the days before I reported to college I would accompany my grandma to the kitchen to cook. This was the period that I perfected my art of cooking. I was so proud when one day I made dinner for the family and grandma said that it was delicious.

When I went to college I did not cook many times. For the times I cooked, the food did not come out delicious like grandma's. I felt like there was something missing. I had thought it to myself that I had become a great cook but I had not lived up to my own expectations. I did not use a slow cooker to cook and I thought maybe that was the reason that my meals were not as delicious as grandma's.

I saved and bought a slow cooker while in my second year and this greatly improved the outcome of the food I cooked; it tasted better than before. I had little space for my kitchen which made wish I'd get kitchen appliances that are multipurpose and would save me space.

One day during the summer, at a home appliances exhibition, I came across Instant Pot multicooker slow cooker. I had never seen such a kitchen appliance in my entire life. The first person I thought of after I got to know the Instant Pot multicooker slow cooker was my grandma. This appliance would be so ideal for her and I knew that she would love it. However, now that I'd take long before I visited her I decided to buy it for myself and be using it just to feel the cooking experience of using it.

I bought the Instant Pot multicooker slow cooker after two weeks of knowing about it. I must confess that this is still the best kitchen appliance that I have ever owned. It helped me save on the kitchen space as it is multipurpose. After buying it, I can even count the number of days that I didn't cook for myself. The food was always delicious and it reminded of grandma. I could leave the food cooking and attend to my days' errands and come back to some nice meal.

Fast-forward to the holidays. I bought Instant Pot multicooker slow cooker for grandma and she was very delighted. She told me that she wished that the Instant Pot multicooker slow cooker would have earlier because it was multipurpose unlike her ordinary old slow cooker. It's now more than a year since I bought her the Instant Pot multicooker slow cooker and she still thanks me.

The Instant Pot multicooker slow cooker is not like ordinary slow cooker; it is a special type with multiple cooking functions and has many other feature that will make your cooking fun. It does not have a pressure cooker function, but has other smart cooking functions such as stew, yogurt, steam, bake, sear/sauté, rice, slow cook, roast, warm and ferment.

Slow cooking is one of the healthiest ways of cooking tasty and delicious food. This slow cooker is easy to use and does not need special skills to operate them. The cleaning process is also easy you never need to spend the whole day on cleaning process.

The purpose of this book is to help you prepare recipes that delicious and tasty using the Instant Pot multicooker slow cooker and enjoy the many benefits that come with this kitchen appliance. The recipes in this book are prepared the Instant Pot multicooker slow cooker with which you can cook any type of meal on varying low temperatures for hours. There are many different meals that only taste great when prepared at low temperatures for longer durations. In this cookbook, you can find all the delicious recipes that you can cook the Instant Pot multicooker slow cooker. The recipes are easy to make and the ingredients can be easily found at the stores.

Get yourself this kitchen appliance and you will live to love it and the meals it prepares.

Happy reading!

CHAPTER 1 BREAKFASTS AND BRUNCHES

Irish Steel Cut Oatmeal

Prep time: 5 minutes | **Cook time:** 3 to 4 hours | **Serves** 8

- 2 tablespoons unsalted butter
- 2 cups steel-cut oats
- 8 cups water
- 1 teaspoon salt

1. Melt butter in a skillet over medium heat. Add oats and toast, stirring constantly, until golden and fragrant, about 2 minutes. Transfer to a slow cooker.
2. Stir water and salt into a slow cooker. Cover and cook until oats are softened and thickened, press the Slow Cook button, and cook on high for 3 to 4 hours. (Press Slow Cook again to toggle between Low and High cooking temperatures.) Stir oatmeal to recombine. Turn off slow cooker and let oatmeal sit for 10 minutes. Serve. (Oatmeal can be refrigerated for up to 4 days. Reheat oatmeal in microwave or in saucepan over medium-low heat; stir often and adjust consistency with hot water as needed.)

Sweet Potato and Corn Scramble

Prep time: 10 minutes | **Cook time:** 8 hours | **Serves** 2

- 1 teaspoon butter, at room temperature, or extra-virgin olive oil
- 4 eggs
- ½ cup 2% milk
- ⅛ teaspoon sea salt
- ½ teaspoon smoked paprika
- ½ teaspoon ground cumin
- Freshly ground black pepper, to taste
- 1 cup finely diced sweet potato
- 1 cup frozen corn kernels, thawed
- ½ cup diced roasted red peppers
- 2 tablespoons minced onion

1. Grease the inside of the slow cooker with the butter.
2. In a small bowl, whisk together the eggs, milk, salt, paprika, and cumin. Season with the freshly ground black pepper.
3. Put the sweet potato, corn, red peppers, and onion into the slow cooker. Pour in the egg mixture and stir gently.
4. Cover and press the Slow Cook button, and cook on low for 8 hours or overnight. (Press Slow Cook again to toggle between Low and High cooking temperatures.) Serve warm.

Cheese and Ham Breakfast Soufflé

Prep time: 10 minutes | **Cook time:** 3 to 4 hours | **Serves** 6

- 8 slices bread (crusts removed), cubed or torn into squares
- 2 cups shredded Cheddar, Swiss, or American cheese
- 1 cup cooked, chopped ham
- 4 eggs
- 1 cup light cream or milk
- 1 cup evaporated milk
- ¼ teaspoon salt
- 1 tablespoon parsley
- Paprika, to taste
- Nonstick cooking spray

1. Lightly grease a slow cooker with nonstick cooking spray. Alternate layers of bread and cheese and ham.
2. Beat together eggs, milk, salt, and parsley in a bowl.
3. Pour over bread in a slow cooker and sprinkle with paprika.
4. Cover and press the Slow Cook button, and cook on low for 3 to 4 hours. (Press Slow Cook again to toggle between Low and High cooking temperatures.) (The longer cooking time yields a firmer, dryer dish.)
5. Serve warm.

Fish Congee

Prep time: 10 minutes | **Cook time:** 4⅓ hours | **Serves** 6

- 1½ cups long-grain white rice
- 1 (1-inch) piece fresh ginger, peeled and grated
- 3 quarts boiling water
- 12 ounces (340 g) firm white fish fillets, such as flounder or cod, skin removed, thinly sliced
- Coarse salt, to taste
- Sliced scallions, for serving

1. Place the rice and ginger into the slow cooker. Add the boiling water and stir. Cover and press the Slow Cook button, and cook on low for about 4 hours or on high for 2 hours until congee reaches consistency of loose porridge. (Press Slow Cook again to toggle between Low and High cooking temperatures.)
2. Add fish and cook on low until fish falls apart, about 20 minutes more (or on high for 10 minutes). Season to taste with salt and serve with the sliced scallions.

Almond and Date Oatmeal

Prep time: 5 minutes | **Cook time:** 4 to 6 hours | **Serves** 8

- 2 cups dry rolled oats
- ½ cup dry Grape-Nuts cereal
- ½ cup slivered almonds
- ¼ cup chopped dates
- 4 cups water

1. Combine all ingredients in a slow cooker. Press the Slow Cook button, and cook on low for 4 to 6 hours. (Press Slow Cook again to toggle between Low and High cooking temperatures.)
2. Serve with fat-free milk, if desired.

Western Omelet Bake

Prep time: 15 minutes | **Cook time:** 8 to 9 hours | **Serves** 10

- 1 (32-ounce / 907-g) bag frozen hash brown potatoes
- 1 pound (454 g) cooked ham, cubed
- 1 medium onion, diced
- 1½ cups shredded Cheddar cheese
- 12 eggs
- 1 cup milk
- 1 teaspoon salt
- 1 teaspoon pepper

1. Layer one-third each of frozen potatoes, ham, onion, and cheese in the bottom of the slow cooker. Repeat 2 times.
2. Beat together eggs, milk, salt, and pepper in a bowl.
3. Pour over mixture in a slow cooker. Cover and press the Slow Cook button, and cook on low for 8 to 9 hours. (Press Slow Cook again to toggle between Low and High cooking temperatures.)
4. Serve with orange juice and fresh fruit, if desired.

Ricotta and Spinach Egg Bake

Prep time: 15 minutes | **Cook time:** 2 to 3 hours | **Serves** 4

- 1 onion, finely chopped
- 1 tablespoon extra-virgin olive oil
- 3 garlic cloves, minced
- 10 ounces (283 g) whole-milk ricotta cheese
- 8 ounces (227 g) frozen chopped spinach, thawed and squeezed dry
- 4 ounces (113 g) fontina cheese, shredded
- 4 large eggs, lightly beaten
- ¼ teaspoon salt
- ¼ teaspoon pepper
- 2 plum tomatoes, cored and sliced crosswise ¼ inch thick

1. Microwave onion, oil, and garlic in a large bowl, stirring occasionally, until onion is softened, about 5 minutes. Stir in ricotta, spinach, fontina, eggs, salt, and pepper until well combined. Divide mixture evenly among four greased ramekins and scatter tomatoes over top.
2. Fill a slow cooker with ½ inch boiling water (about 2 cups water) and set ramekins in the slow cooker. Cover and press the Slow Cook button, and cook on low for 2 to 3 hours or until the eggs are set . (Press Slow Cook again to toggle between Low and High cooking temperatures.) Using tongs and sturdy spatula, remove ramekins from slow cooker and let cool for 15 minutes before serving.

CHAPTER 2 APPETIZERS

Simple Spiced Nuts

Prep time: 5 minutes | **Cook time:** 2 to 3 hours | **Serves** 10 to 14

- 1 large egg white
- 1 tablespoon water
- 1 teaspoon salt
- 3 cups whole unblanched almonds, cashews, pecans, or walnuts
- ¼ cup sugar
- 2 teaspoons ground cinnamon
- 1 teaspoon ground ginger
- 1 teaspoon ground coriander
- Vegetable oil spray

1. Lightly coat slow cooker with vegetable oil spray. Whisk egg white, water, and salt together in a large bowl. Add almonds and toss to coat, then drain thoroughly in a fine-mesh strainer.
2. Combine sugar, cinnamon, ginger, and coriander in a separate large bowl. Add almonds and toss to coat. Transfer almond mixture to prepared slow cooker, cover, and and press the Slow Cook button, and cook on high for 2 to 3 hours or until almonds are toasted and fragrant, stirring every 30 minutes. (Press Slow Cook again to toggle between Low and High cooking temperatures.)
3. Transfer almond mixture to a rimmed baking sheet and spread into an even layer. Let cool to room temperature, about 20 minutes. Serve immediately. (Almonds can be stored at room temperature for up to 1 week.)

Sweet and Spicy Peanuts

Prep time: 10 minutes | **Cook time:** 1½ hours | Makes 4 cups

- 3 cups salted peanuts
- ½ cup sugar
- ⅓ cup packed brown sugar
- 2 tablespoons hot water
- 2 tablespoons butter, melted
- 1 tablespoon Sriracha Asian hot chili sauce or hot pepper sauce
- 1 teaspoon chili powder

1. Place peanuts in a greased slow cooker. In a small bowl, combine the sugars, water, butter, hot sauce, and chili powder. Pour over peanuts and stir to coat. Cover and press the Slow Cook button, and cook on high for 1½ hours. (Press Slow Cook again to toggle between Low and High cooking temperatures.), stirring once.
2. Spread on waxed paper to cool. Serve warm.

Barbecue Sausage Bites

Prep time: 10 minutes | **Cook time:** 1 to 2 hours | **Serves** 8 to 10

- 1 cup ketchup
- ½ cup molasses
- 3 tablespoons cider vinegar
- 3 tablespoons Dijon mustard
- 1 tablespoon packed brown sugar
- 2 teaspoons chili powder
- ⅛ teaspoon cayenne pepper
- 3 pounds (1.4 kg) kielbasa sausage, sliced on bias ½ inch thick

1. Combine ketchup, molasses, vinegar, mustard, sugar, chili powder, and cayenne in the slow cooker.
2. Stir in kielbasa, cover, and press the Slow Cook button, and cook on low for 1 to 2 hours or until heated through and flavors meld. (Press Slow Cook again to toggle between Low and High cooking temperatures.) Serve. (Kielbasa can be held on warm or low setting for up to 2 hours. Adjust sauce consistency with hot water as needed, adding 2 tablespoons at a time.)

Lemony Chicken Wings

Prep time: 15 minutes | **Cook time:** 6 to 8 hours | **Makes** about 4 dozen

- 5 pounds (2.3 kg) chicken wings (about 25 wings)
- 1 (12-ounce / 340-g) bottle chili sauce
- ¼ cup lemon juice
- ¼ cup molasses
- 2 tablespoons Worcestershire sauce
- 6 garlic cloves, minced
- 1 tablespoon chili powder
- 1 tablespoon salsa
- 1 teaspoon garlic salt
- 3 drops hot pepper sauce

1. Cut chicken wings into three sections, discarding wing tips. Place the wings in a slow cooker.
2. In a small bowl, combine the remaining ingredients. Pour over chicken and stir to coat. Cover and press the Slow Cook button, and cook on low for 6 to 8 hours or until chicken is tender. (Press Slow Cook again to toggle between Low and High cooking temperatures.) Serve warm.

Beef and Green Olive Dip

Prep time: 15 minutes | **Cook time:** 3 to 4 hours | **Makes** 8 cups

- 1 pound (454 g) ground beef
- 1 medium sweet red pepper, chopped
- 1 small onion, chopped
- 1 (16-ounce / 454-g) can refried beans
- 1 (16-ounce / 454-g) jar mild salsa
- 2 cups (8 ounces / 227 g) shredded part-skim Mozzarella cheese
- 2 cups (8 ounces / 227 g) shredded Cheddar cheese
- 1 (5¾-ounce / 163-g) jar sliced green olives with pimientos, drained
- Tortilla chips, for serving

1. In a large skillet, cook the beef, pepper and onion over medium heat until meat is no longer pink, about 6 to 8 minutes. Drain.
2. Transfer the beef mixture to a greased slow cooker. Stir in the beans, salsa, cheeses and olives. Cover and press the Slow Cook button, and cook on low for 3 to 4 hours or until cheese is melted, stirring occasionally. (Press Slow Cook again to toggle between Low and High cooking temperatures.) Serve with chips.

Grape Jelly Meatballs

Prep time: 10 minutes | **Cook time:** 4 to 5 hours | **Makes** about 10½ dozen

- 1 cup grape juice
- 1 cup apple jelly
- 1 cup ketchup
- 1 (8-ounce / 227-g) can tomato sauce
- 1 (64-ounce / 1.8-kg) package frozen fully cooked Italian meatballs

1. In a small saucepan, combine the juice, jelly, ketchup, and tomato sauce. Cook and stir over medium heat until jelly is melted.
2. Place the meatballs in a slow cooker. Pour the sauce over the top and gently stir to coat. Cover and press the Slow Cook button, and cook on low for 4 to 5 hours or until heated through. (Press Slow Cook again to toggle between Low and High cooking temperatures.) Serve warm.

Turkey Teriyaki Sandwiches

Prep time: 20 minutes | **Cook time:** 5¾ to 6¾ hours | **Serves** 20

- 2 boneless skinless turkey breast halves (2 pounds / 907 g each)
- $^{2}/_{3}$ cup packed brown sugar
- $^{2}/_{3}$ cup reduced-sodium soy sauce
- ¼ cup cider vinegar
- 3 garlic cloves, minced
- 1 tablespoon minced fresh ginger
- ½ teaspoon pepper
- 2 tablespoons cornstarch
- 2 tablespoons cold water
- 20 Hawaiian sweet rolls
- 2 tablespoons butter, melted

1. Place turkey in a slow cooker. In a small bowl, combine the brown sugar, soy sauce, vinegar, garlic, ginger, and pepper. Pour over turkey and stir to coat. Cover and press the Slow Cook button, and cook on low for 5 to 6 hours or until meat is tender. (Press Slow Cook again to toggle between Low and High cooking temperatures.)
2. Remove turkey from the slow cooker. In another bowl, mix cornstarch and cold water until smooth. Gradually stir the mixture into cooking liquid. When cool enough to handle, shred meat with two forks and return meat to a slow cooker. Cover and press the Slow Cook button, and cook on high for 30 to 35 minutes or until sauce is thickened. (Press Slow Cook again to toggle between Low and High cooking temperatures.)
3. Preheat the oven to 325ºF (163ºC). Split rolls and brush cut sides with butter, then place on a baking sheet, cut side up. Bake for 8 to 10 minutes or until toasted and golden brown. Spoon $^{1}/_{3}$ cup turkey mixture on roll bottoms. Replace tops and serve.

Turkey Meatballs with Garlic and Pesto

Prep time: 10 minutes | **Cook time:** 4 to 5 hours | **Serves** 12 to 14

- 4 cups lightly packed fresh basil leaves
- 4 garlic cloves, minced
- 1/3 cup extra-virgin olive oil
- 2 ounces (57 g) Parmesan cheese, grated (1 cup)
- 1 1/3 cups panko bread crumbs
- 2 large egg yolks
- Salt and pepper, to taste
- 2 pounds (907 g) ground turkey
- 1 (28-ounce / 794-g) can crushed tomatoes
- Vegetable oil spray

1. Preheat the oven to 475ºF (245ºC). Set a wire rack in aluminum foil-lined rimmed baking sheet and coat with vegetable oil spray. Set aside.
2. Process basil and garlic in a food processor until finely ground, about 30 seconds, scraping down sides of bowl as needed. With processor running, slowly add oil and process until smooth, about 30 seconds. Measure out and reserve 2 tablespoons of pesto for serving. Transfer remaining pesto to a large bowl.
3. Stir Parmesan, panko, egg yolks, ½ teaspoon salt, and ¼ teaspoon pepper into remaining pesto. Add ground turkey and knead with hands until well combined. Pinch off and roll turkey mixture into tablespoon-size meatballs (about 60 meatballs) and arrange on the prepared rack. Bake in the preheated oven until no longer pink, about 10 minutes. Transfer meatballs to slow cooker.
4. Gently stir tomatoes and ½ teaspoon salt into a slow cooker, cover, and press the Slow Cook button, and cook on low for 4 to 5 hours or until meatballs are tender. (Press Slow Cook again to toggle between Low and High cooking temperatures.)
5. Using a large spoon, skim excess fat from surface of sauce. Stir reserved pesto into meatballs and season with salt and pepper to taste. Serve. (Meatballs can be held on warm or low setting for up to 2 hours. Adjust sauce consistency with hot water as needed, adding 2 tablespoons at a time.)

CHAPTER 3 STOCKS AND SAUCES

Chicken Stock

Prep time: 20 minutes | **Cook time:** 8 hours | **Makes** 4 to 5 quarts

- 2 to 3 pounds (907 g to 1.4 kg) chicken bones
- 2 carrots, chopped
- 2 onions, quartered
- 3 celery stalks, chopped
- 1 leek, split lengthwise, rinsed well, and chopped
- 1 head garlic, cut in half
- 1 dried bay leaf
- 1 tablespoon black peppercorns
- 3 thyme sprigs
- 5 flat-leaf parsley sprigs
- 3 to 4 quarts boiling water

1. Place all ingredients except boiling water in a slow cooker. Add the boiling water (it should cover the ingredients by 3 inches). Cover and press the Slow Cook button, and cook on low for 8 hours. (Press Slow Cook again to toggle between Low and High cooking temperatures.).
2. Remove from heat and strain stock through a fine-mesh sieve (discard solids). Let stock cool completely. (Stock can be refrigerated in an airtight container for up to 1 week, or frozen for up to 6 months.)

Garlic Fresh Tomato Sauce

Prep time: 10 minutes | **Cook time:** 5 hours | **Makes** about 3 cups

- 2 pounds (907 g) ripe plum tomatoes, peeled cored, halved, and seeded
- 4 garlic cloves, smashed and peeled
- ¼ cup extra-virgin olive oil
- 4 to 5 basil sprigs
- 1 teaspoon coarse salt, plus more to taste
- ¼ teaspoon freshly ground pepper
- Pinch sugar
- ½ cup boiling water

1. Add tomatoes, garlic, oil, basil, salt, pepper, and sugar to a slow cooker. Stir to combine. Add the boiling water. Cover and press the Slow Cook button, and cook on high for 1 hour until sauce thickens slightly. Cook on low for 4 hours more. (Press Slow Cook again to toggle between Low and High cooking temperatures.)
2. For a thicker sauce, continue cooking on low for 2 hours, or until desired thickness is reached. Serve sauce immediately, or let cool to room temperature and refrigerate in an airtight container for up to 3 days.

Italian Beef Sauce

Prep time: 20 minutes | **Cook time:** 6 to 8 hours | **Makes** 8 to 9 cups

- ½ cup olive oil
- 2 medium-size yellow onions, chopped
- 2 medium-size carrots, finely chopped
- 2 ribs celery, finely chopped
- 1 pound (454 g) lean ground beef
- Salt and freshly ground black pepper, to taste
- 1½ cups dry red wine, such as Chianti
- 2 (28-ounce / 794-g) cans whole plum tomatoes, with their juice; or 2 pounds (907 g) fresh ripe plum tomatoes, peeled, deseeded, and cut into chunks
- 1 (6-ounce / 170-g) can tomato paste
- ½ cup beef broth

1. Heat the oil in a large skillet over medium heat. Cook the onions, carrots, and celery, stirring occasionally, until just browned, 10 to 15 minutes. Add the beef and cook until no longer pink. Season with salt and pepper.
2. Transfer to the slow cooker. Add the wine to the skillet over high heat and cook, scraping up any browned bits stuck to the bottom, until it reduces to half its volume. Pour into the slow cooker and add the tomatoes, tomato paste, and broth. Cover and press the Slow Cook button, and cook on low for 6 to 8 hours. (Press Slow Cook again to toggle between Low and High cooking temperatures.) Serve the sauce hot. It will keep in the refrigerator for up to 4 days and in the freezer for a month.

Vegan Garlic Pasta Sauce

Prep time: 20 minutes | **Cook time:** 4 hours | **Makes** 8 cups

- 2 tablespoon extra-virgin olive oil
- 2 cloves garlic, minced
- ½ teaspoon red pepper flakes
- 1 large onion, coarsely chopped
- 2 portobello mushrooms, coarsely chopped
- 1 medium red bell pepper, deseeded and coarsely chopped
- 1 medium yellow bell pepper, deseeded and coarsely chopped
- 1 tablespoon dried oregano
- 2 teaspoons dried basil
- Salt, to taste
- 2 tablespoons balsamic vinegar
- 2 (32-ounce / 907-g) cans crushed plum tomatoes
- Freshly ground black pepper, to taste

1. Heat the oil in a large sauté pan over medium-high heat. Add the garlic and red pepper flakes, and sauté until the garlic is fragrant, about 1 minute. Add the onion and sauté until the onion begins to soften, another 2 minutes. Add the remaining vegetables, the oregano, basil, and 2 teaspoons of salt and sauté until the vegetables give off some liquid, about 5 minutes.
2. Using a slotted spoon, transfer the vegetables to a slow cooker. Stir in the vinegar and tomatoes. Cover and press the Slow Cook button, and cook on high for 4 hours or on low for 8 hours. (Press Slow Cook again to toggle between Low and High cooking temperatures.) Season with salt and pepper.
3. Serve immediately or refrigerate until ready to serve.

Berry Sauce

Prep time: 10 minutes | **Cook time:** 4 hours | **Makes** about 10 cups

- 2 pints fresh blackberries
- 2 pints fresh strawberries, hulled, cut into quarters if large
- 2 pints fresh blueberries, picked over for stems
- 1 to 1½ cups sugar (depending on the sweetness of the berries)
- 2 tablespoons fresh lemon juice
- Grated zest of 1 lemon
- 2 tablespoons cornstarch

1. Mix all the ingredients together in a slow cooker. Cover and press the Slow Cook button, and cook on low for 4 hours, stirring twice during the cooking time. (Press Slow Cook again to toggle between Low and High cooking temperatures.)
2. Allow the sauce to cool before removing from the cooker. Store in airtight containers in the refrigerator for up to 1 week or in the freezer for up to 3 months.

CHAPTER 4 DESSERTS

Spiced Pear and Almond Crumble

Prep time: 10 minutes | **Cook time:** 2½ hours | **Serves** 8

- 1 cup firmly packed light brown sugar
- ¼ cup amaretto liqueur
- ¾ cup (1½ sticks) unsalted butter, melted
- 8 large firm pears, peeled, cored and coarsely chopped
- ½ cup granulated sugar
- ½ cup all-purpose flour
- ¾ teaspoon ground cinnamon
- ¼ teaspoon freshly grated nutmeg
- ⅔ cup sliced almonds
- Nonstick cooking spray
- Whipped cream, for serving

1. Coat the insert of a slow cooker with nonstick cooking spray. Add the brown sugar, amaretto, and ½ cup of the butter to the slow cooker and stir until blended. Add the pears and turn the pears to coat with the syrup.
2. Stir together the granulated sugar, flour, cinnamon, nutmeg, and almonds in a small bowl. Drizzle the remaining ¼ cup butter into the flour mixture and stir with a fork until the mixture begins to form crumbs. Sprinkle over the top of the pears. Cover and press the Slow Cook button, and cook on high for 2½ hours or until a skewer inserted into the crumble comes out clean. (Press Slow Cook again to toggle between Low and High cooking temperatures.) Uncover and allow to cool for 30 minutes.
3. Serve the crumble warm with a dollop of whipped cream.

Raisin Rice Pudding

Prep time: 10 minutes | **Cook time:** 2 hours | **Serves** 6

- 2½ cups rice, cooked
- 1½ cups evaporated milk or scalded milk
- ⅔ cup brown or white sugar
- 1 tablespoon butter, softened
- 2 teaspoons vanilla
- ½ to 1 teaspoon nutmeg
- 1 eggs, beaten
- ½ to 1 cup raisins

1. Mix together all ingredients in a bowl. Pour into lightly greased slow cooker.
2. Cover and press the Slow Cook button, and cook on high for 2 hours or on low for 4 to 6 hours. (Press Slow Cook again to toggle between Low and High cooking temperatures.) Stir after first hour.
3. Serve warm or cold.

Pecan and Butterscotch Bread Pudding

Prep time: 15 minutes | **Cook time:** 3 to 4 hours | **Serves** 8

- 9 cups cubed day-old white bread (about 8 slices)
- ½ cup chopped pecans
- ½ cup butterscotch chips
- 4 eggs
- 2 cups half-and-half
- ½ cup packed brown sugar
- ½ cup butter, melted
- 1 teaspoon vanilla extract
- Whipped cream and butterscotch ice cream topping, for serving

1. Place bread, pecans, and butterscotch chips in a greased slow cooker. In a large bowl, whisk eggs, half-and-half, brown sugar, melted butter, and vanilla until blended. Pour over bread mixture, stirring gently to combine.
2. Cook, covered, press the Slow Cook button, and cook on low for 3 to 4 hours or until a knife inserted in center comes out clean. (Press Slow Cook again to toggle between Low and High cooking temperatures.) Serve warm with whipped cream and butterscotch topping.

Baked Cinnamon Apples

Prep time: 10 minutes | **Cook time:** 3 to 4 hours | **Serves** 7

- 6 large tart apples
- 2 tablespoons lemon juice
- ½ cup packed brown sugar
- ½ cup sugar
- 2 tablespoons all-purpose flour
- 1 teaspoon ground cinnamon
- ¼ teaspoon ground nutmeg
- 6 tablespoons butter, melted
- Vanilla ice cream, for serving

1. Peel, core and cut each apple into eight wedges. Transfer the wedges to a slow cooker. Drizzle with lemon juice.
2. Combine the sugars, flour, cinnamon, and nutmeg in a bowl. Sprinkle the mixture over apples and drizzle with butter.
3. Cover and press the Slow Cook button, and cook on low for 3 to 4 hours or until apples are tender. (Press Slow Cook again to toggle between Low and High cooking temperatures.) Serve in dessert dishes with ice cream.

Creamy Pumpkin Pie Pudding

Prep time: 10 minutes | **Cook time:** 3 hours | **Serves** 8

- 1 (15-ounce / 425-g) can pumpkin
- 1 (12-ounce / 340-g) can evaporated skim milk
- ¾ cup Splenda
- ½ cup low-fat buttermilk baking mix
- 2 eggs, beaten, or 6 egg whites
- 2 teaspoons pumpkin pie spice
- 1 teaspoon lemon zest
- Cooking spray

1. Combine all ingredients in a slow cooker sprayed with cooking spray. Stir until lumps disappear.
2. Cover and press the Slow Cook button, and cook on low for 3 hours. (Press Slow Cook again to toggle between Low and High cooking temperatures.)
3. Serve warm or cold.

Fallen Chocolate Soufflé Cake

Prep time: 5 minutes | **Cook time:** 6 hours | **Serves** 10 to 12

- 1 (18¼-ounce / 517-g) package chocolate cake mix
- ½ cup vegetable oil
- 2 cups sour cream
- 4 eggs, beaten
- 1 (3-ounce / 85-g) box instant chocolate pudding mix
- 1 cup chocolate chips (optional)

1. Combine all ingredients in a greased slow cooker.
2. Cover and press the Slow Cook button, and cook on low for 6 hours. (Press Slow Cook again to toggle between Low and High cooking temperatures.) (Do not lift the lid until the end of the cooking time!)
3. Insert a toothpick into the center of cake to see if it comes out clean. If it does, the soufflé is finished. If it doesn't, continue cooking for another 15 minutes. Check again. Repeat until it's finished cooking.
4. Serve warm.

Fruity Cake with Walnuts

Prep time: 10 minutes | **Cook time:** 3 to 5 hours | **Serves** 10 to 12

- 1 or 2 (21-ounce / 595-g) cans apple, blueberry, or peach pie filling
- 1 (18¼-ounce / 517-g) package yellow cake mix
- 1 stick (½ cup) butter, melted
- ⅓ cup chopped walnuts
- Nonstick cooking spray

1. Spray the insert of the slow cooker with nonstick cooking spray.
2. Place pie filling in a slow cooker.
3. In a mixing bowl, combine dry cake mix and butter. Spoon over filling.
4. Drop walnuts over top.
5. Cover and press the Slow Cook button, and cook on low for 3 to 5 hours or until a toothpick inserted into the center of topping comes out clean. (Press Slow Cook again to toggle between Low and High cooking temperatures.) Serve warm.

Apple Pie Oatmeal

Prep time: 10 minutes | **Cook time:** 4 to 5 hours | **Serves** 6

- 1 cup quick-cooking oats
- ½ cup all-purpose flour
- ⅓ cup packed brown sugar
- 2 teaspoons baking powder
- 1½ teaspoons apple pie spice
- ¼ teaspoon salt
- 3 eggs
- 1⅔ cups 2% milk, divided
- 1½ teaspoons vanilla extract
- 3 medium apples, peeled and finely chopped
- Vanilla ice cream (optional)

1. In a large bowl, whisk oats, flour, brown sugar, baking powder, pie spice and salt. In a small bowl, whisk eggs, 1 cup milk and vanilla until blended. Add to oat mixture, stirring just until moistened. Fold in apples.
2. Transfer to a greased slow cooker. Cover and press the Slow Cook button, and cook on low for 4 to 5 hours or until apples are tender and top is set. (Press Slow Cook again to toggle between Low and High cooking temperatures.)
3. Stir in remaining milk. Serve warm or cold with ice cream if desired.

Coconut Bananas Foster

Prep time: 10 minutes | **Cook time:** 2 hours | **Serves** 5

- 5 medium firm bananas
- 1 cup packed brown sugar
- ¼ cup butter, melted
- ¼ cup rum
- 1 teaspoon vanilla extract
- ½ teaspoon ground cinnamon
- ⅓ cup chopped walnuts
- ⅓ cup flaked coconut
- Vanilla ice cream or sliced pound cake, for serving

1. Cut bananas in half lengthwise, then widthwise. Layer in the bottom of a slow cooker. Combine the brown sugar, butter, rum, vanilla, and cinnamon, then pour over bananas. Cover and press the Slow Cook button, and cook on low for 1½ hours or until heated through. (Press Slow Cook again to toggle between Low and High cooking temperatures.)
2. Sprinkle with walnuts and coconut and cook for 30 minutes longer. Serve with ice cream or pound cake.

Simple Pineapple Tapioca

Prep time: 10 minutes | **Cook time:** 3 hours | **Serves** 4 to 6

- 2½ cups water
- 2½ cups pineapple juice
- ½ cup dry small pearl tapioca
- ¾ to 1 cup sugar
- 1 (15-ounce / 425-g) can crushed pineapple, undrained

1. Mix first four ingredients together in a slow cooker.
2. Cover and press the Slow Cook button, and cook on high for 3 hours. (Press Slow Cook again to toggle between Low and High cooking temperatures.)
3. Stir in crushed pineapple. Chill for several hours before serving.

Cinnamon Applesauce

Prep time: 10 minutes | **Cook time:** 8 to 10 hours | **Serves** 8 to 10

- 8 apples, peeled, cored, and cut into chunks or slices (6 cups)
- 1 teaspoon cinnamon
- ½ cup water
- ½ to 1 cup sugar

1. Combine all ingredients in a slow cooker.
2. Cover and press the Slow Cook button, and cook on low for 8 to 10 hours or on high for 3 to 4 hours. (Press Slow Cook again to toggle between Low and High cooking temperatures.) Serve warm.

Vanilla Creme Brûlée

Prep time: 5 minutes | **Cook time:** 2 to 3 hours | **Serves** 4

- 2 cups heavy cream
- 5 large egg yolks
- ⅓ cup granulated sugar
- 1 teaspoon vanilla extract
- Pinch salt
- 4 teaspoons turbinado or Demerara sugar

1. Whisk cream, egg yolks, granulated sugar, vanilla, and salt in a bowl until sugar has dissolved. Strain custard through a fine-mesh strainer into a 4-cup liquid measuring cup. Divide custard evenly among four 6-ounce / 170-g ramekins. Fill a slow cooker with ½ inch water (about 2 cups) and set ramekins in a slow cooker. Cover and cook until centers are just barely set and register 185ºF (85ºC), press the Slow Cook button, and cook on low for 2 to 3 hours. (Press Slow Cook again to toggle between Low and High cooking temperatures.)
2. Using tongs and sturdy spatula, transfer ramekins to a wire rack and let cool to room temperature, about 2 hours. Cover with plastic wrap and refrigerate until well chilled, at least for 4 hours or up to 2 days.
3. To serve, gently blot away condensation using paper towels. Sprinkle each ramekin with 1 teaspoon turbinado sugar. Tilt and tap each ramekin to distribute sugar evenly, then dump out excess sugar and wipe rims of ramekins clean. Ignite torch and caramelize sugar. Refrigerate ramekins, uncovered, to re-chill custard before serving, 30 to 45 minutes.

Strawberry Rhubarb Crisp

Prep time: 20 minutes | **Cook time:** 2½ hours | **Serves** 8

- 4 cups strawberries, hulled and cut into quarters
- 4 stalks bright red rhubarb, cut into ½-inch slices
- 1½ cups granulated sugar
- 1 teaspoon ground cinnamon
- Grated zest of 1 orange
- 1 tablespoon cornstarch
- ⅔ cup old-fashioned rolled oats
- ¾ cup firmly packed light brown sugar
- ½ cup finely chopped white chocolate
- 1 cup all-purpose flour
- ½ cup (1 stick) unsalted butter, chilled and cut into ½-inch pieces
- Nonstick cooking spray
- Vanilla ice cream, for serving

1. Coat the insert of a slow cooker with nonstick cooking spray. Stir the berries, rhubarb, granulated sugar, cinnamon, zest, and cornstarch together in the insert. Set aside while making the crumble.
2. Stir together the oats, brown sugar, chocolate, and flour in a mixing bowl. Add the butter and cut the butter into the dry ingredients, using a blending fork or pastry blender, until the mixture forms coarse crumbs about the size of peas.
3. Sprinkle the crumble over the fruit. Cover and press the Slow Cook button, and cook on low for 2½ hours, until the crumble is set, and the fruit is bubbling. (Press Slow Cook again to toggle between Low and High cooking temperatures.) Uncover the slow cooker and allow to cool for 30 minutes.
4. Serve warm with vanilla ice cream.

Lemon Blueberry Cornmeal Cake

Prep time: 10 minutes | **Cook time:** 2 to 3 hours | **Serves** 6

- 1 cup all-purpose flour
- ¼ cup cornmeal
- ½ teaspoon baking powder
- ½ teaspoon baking soda
- Salt, to taste
- ½ cup plain yogurt
- ⅓ cup granulated sugar
- 1 large egg
- 2 teaspoons grated lemon zest plus 4 teaspoons juice
- ½ teaspoon vanilla extract
- 4 tablespoons unsalted butter, melted
- 5 ounces (142 g) blueberries
- ¾ cup confectioners' sugar
- Cooking spray

1. Fill a slow cooker with ½ inch water (about 2 cups) and place aluminum foil rack in bottom. Make foil sling for 8½ by 4½-inch loaf pan by folding 2 long sheets of foil; first sheet should be 8½ inches wide and second sheet should be 4½ inches wide. Lay sheets of foil in a pan perpendicular to each other, with extra foil hanging over edges of pan. Push foil into corners and up sides of pan, smoothing foil flush to pan. Lightly grease foil with cooking spray.
2. Whisk flour, cornmeal, baking powder, baking soda, and ½ teaspoon of salt together in a bowl. In a large bowl, whisk yogurt, granulated sugar, egg, lemon zest, and vanilla until smooth, then slowly whisk in melted butter until well combined. Stir in flour mixture until just incorporated. Gently fold in blueberries.
3. Scrape batter into prepared pan and smooth top. Gently tap pan on the counter to release air bubbles. Set pan on prepared rack, cover, and press the Slow Cook button, and cook on high for 2 to 3 hours. (Press Slow Cook again to toggle between Low and High cooking temperatures.) Cook until toothpick inserted in center comes out clean.
4. Let cake cool in pan on wire rack for 10 minutes. Using foil overhang, lift cake out of pan and transfer to rack, discarding foil. Let cake cool completely, 1 to 2 hours.
5. Whisk confectioners' sugar, pinch salt, and lemon juice in a small bowl until smooth. Flip cake over onto a serving dish. Drizzle top and sides with glaze and let glaze set before serving, about 25 minutes.

Creamy Cheesecake

Prep time: 10 minutes | **Cook time:** 1½ to 2½ hours | **Serves** 8

- 6 whole graham crackers, broken into 1-inch pieces
- 2 tablespoons unsalted butter, melted
- ²/₃ cup plus 1 tablespoon sugar, divided
- ½ teaspoon ground cinnamon
- Salt, to taste
- 18 ounces (510 g) cream cheese, softened
- 1 teaspoon vanilla extract
- ¼ cup sour cream
- 2 large eggs

1. Pulse graham crackers in a food processor to fine crumbs, about 20 pulses. Add melted butter, 1 tablespoon sugar, cinnamon, and pinch salt and pulse to combine, about 4 pulses. Sprinkle crumbs into a springform pan and press into an even layer using the bottom of the dry measuring cup. Wipe out processor bowl.
2. Process cream cheese, vanilla, ¼ teaspoon salt, and remaining ²/₃ cup sugar in the processor until combined, about 15 seconds, scraping down sides of bowl as needed. Add sour cream and eggs and process until just incorporated, about 15 seconds; do not over mix. Pour filling into prepared pan and smooth top.
3. Fill a slow cooker with ½ inch water (about 2 cups) and place aluminum foil rack in bottom. Set pan on prepared rack, cover, and cook until cheesecake registers 150ºF (66ºC), press the Slow Cook button, and cook on high for 1½ to 2½ hours. (Press Slow Cook again to toggle between Low and High cooking temperatures.) Turn off slow cooker and let cheesecake sit, covered, for 1 hour.
4. Transfer cheesecake to a wire rack. Run a small knife around edge of cake and gently blot away condensation using paper towels. Let cheesecake cool in pan to room temperature, about 1 hour. Cover with plastic wrap and refrigerate until well chilled, at least for 3 hours or up to 3 days.
5. About 30 minutes before serving, run a small knife around edge of cheesecake, then remove sides of pan. Invert cheesecake onto sheet of parchment paper, then turn cheesecake right side up onto a serving dish. Serve.

Ginger and Pink Grapefruit Cheesecake

Prep time: 15 minutes | **Cook time:** 2 hours | **Serves** 6

- ¾ cup graham cracker crumbs
- 1 tablespoon plus ⅔ cup sugar, divided
- 1 teaspoon grated grapefruit peel
- ¼ teaspoon ground ginger
- 2½ tablespoons butter, melted
- 2 (8-ounce / 227-g) packages cream cheese, softened
- ½ cup sour cream
- 2 tablespoons pink grapefruit juice
- 2 eggs, lightly beaten

1. Place a greased springform pan on a double thickness of heavy-duty foil. Wrap foil securely around pan. Pour 1 inch water in a slow cooker. Layer two 24-inch pieces of aluminum foil. Starting with a long side, fold up foil to create a 1-inch-wide strip; roll into a coil. Place in a slow cooker to form a rack for the cheesecake.
2. In a small bowl, mix cracker crumbs, 1 tablespoon sugar, peel, and ginger. Stir in butter. Press onto bottom and about 1 inch up sides of prepared pan.
3. In a large bowl, beat cream cheese and remaining sugar until smooth. Beat in sour cream and grapefruit juice. Add eggs and beat on low speed just until combined.
4. Pour into crust. Place springform pan on top of coil. Cover slow cooker with a double layer of paper towels and place lid securely over towels. Cover and press the Slow Cook button, and cook on high for 2 hours. (Press Slow Cook again to toggle between Low and High cooking temperatures.) Do not remove lid. Turn off the slow cooker and let cheesecake stand, covered, in slow cooker for 1 hour. The center of the cheesecake will be just set and the top will appear dull.
5. Remove springform pan from slow cooker and remove foil from pan. Cool cheesecake on a wire rack for 1 hour before serving.

CHAPTER 5 CLASSIC COMFORT FOODS

Mushroom Macaroni and Cheese

Prep time: 20 minutes | **Cook time:** 1 to 2 hours | **Serves** 6 to 8

- 1 pound (454 g) elbow macaroni or small shells
- 1 tablespoon extra-virgin olive oil
- 3 cups boiling water, plus extra as needed
- 2 (12-ounce / 340-g) cans evaporated milk
- 2 (11-ounce / 312-g) cans condensed onion soup
- 8 ounces (227 g) Comté cheese, shredded (2 cups)
- 8 ounces (227 g) Monterey Jack cheese, shredded (2 cups)
- ¼ cup dry white wine
- ¼ ounce (7 g) dried porcini mushrooms, rinsed and minced
- 1 teaspoon dry mustard
- Salt and pepper, to taste
- Vegetable oil spray

1. Line slow cooker with aluminum foil collar and lightly coat with vegetable oil spray. Microwave macaroni and oil in a bowl at 50 percent power, stirring occasionally, until macaroni begin to look toasted and blistered, 5 to 8 minutes.
2. Transfer hot macaroni to prepared slow cooker and immediately stir in 2¾ cups boiling water. Stir in evaporated milk, condensed soup, Comté, Monterey Jack, wine, mushrooms, mustard, 1 teaspoon pepper, and ½ teaspoon salt. Cover and cook until macaroni are tender, press the Slow Cook button, and cook on high for 1 to 2 hours. (Press Slow Cook again to toggle between Low and High cooking temperatures.)
3. Discard foil collar. Gently stir remaining ¼ cup boiling water into macaroni until combined. Season with salt and pepper to taste. Adjust consistency with extra boiling water as needed. Serve. (Macaroni can be held on warm or low setting for up to 30 minutes.)

Ham and Potato Casserole

Prep time: 15 minutes | **Cook time:** 4 to 5 hours | **Serves** 4

- 1 (10¾-ounce / 305-g) can condensed cream of mushroom soup, undiluted
- ½ cup 2% milk
- 1 tablespoon dried parsley flakes
- 6 medium potatoes, peeled and thinly sliced
- 1 small onion, chopped
- 1½ cups cubed fully cooked ham
- 6 slices process American cheese

1. In a small bowl, combine the soup, milk and parsley. In a slow cooker, layer half of the potatoes, onion, ham, cheese, and soup mixture. Repeat layers. Cover and press the Slow Cook button, and cook on low for 4 to 5 hours or until potatoes are tender. (Press Slow Cook again to toggle between Low and High cooking temperatures.) Serve warm.

Farmhouse Chicken Casserole with Carrots

Prep time: 20 minutes | **Cook time:** 4 to 5 hours | **Serves** 6

- 1 pound (454 g) red potatoes, unpeeled and cut into ½-inch pieces
- 3 carrots, peeled, halved lengthwise, and sliced ½ inch thick
- 3 tablespoons extra-virgin olive oil, divided
- ¼ cup chicken broth, plus extra as needed
- 2 tablespoons instant tapioca
- 2 pounds (907 g) boneless, skinless chicken thighs, trimmed
- Salt and pepper, to taste
- 1 (12-inch) baguette, cut into ½-inch pieces
- 1 (5.2-ounce / 147-g) package Boursin Garlic and Fine Herbs cheese, crumbled
- ½ cup frozen peas, thawed

1. Microwave potatoes, carrots, and 1 tablespoon of oil in a covered bowl, stirring occasionally, until vegetables are softened, about 5 minutes; transfer to a slow cooker. Stir in broth and tapioca. Season chicken with salt and pepper and nestle into a slow cooker. Cover and cook until chicken is tender, press the Slow Cook button, and cook on low for 4 to 5 hours. (Press Slow Cook again to toggle between Low and High cooking temperatures.)
2. Preheat the oven to 450ºF (235ºC). Arrange bread in a single layer on rimmed baking sheet and bake until browned and crisp, about 10 minutes, stirring halfway through baking. Toss croutons with remaining 2 tablespoons of oil, and season with salt and pepper to taste. Set aside for serving.
3. Transfer chicken to a cutting board, let cool slightly, then pull apart into large chunks using 2 forks. Stir Boursin into filling until well combined. Stir in chicken and peas and let sit until heated through, about 5 minutes. Adjust consistency with extra hot broth as needed. Season with salt and pepper to taste. Top individual portions with croutons and serve.

Pork and White Bean Stew

Prep time: 25 minutes | **Cook time:** 6 to 8 hours | **Serves** 6 to 8

- 1 (14½-ounce / 411-g) can whole peeled tomatoes
- 2 (15-ounce / 425-g) cans cannellini beans, rinsed
- 2 onions, finely chopped
- 2 slices bacon, finely chopped
- 3 tablespoons tomato paste
- 3 tablespoons minced fresh oregano
- 6 garlic cloves, minced
- Salt and pepper, to taste
- ¼ cup dry white wine
- 8 ounces (227 g) parsnips, peeled and cut into ½-inch pieces
- 4 carrots, peeled and cut into ½-inch pieces
- 1½ pounds (680 g) boneless country-style pork ribs, trimmed and cut into 1½-inch pieces
- 1 (12-inch) baguette, cut into ½-inch pieces
- 2 tablespoons extra-virgin olive oil, plus extra for drizzling

1. Process tomatoes and their juice and half of beans in blender until smooth, about 30 seconds. Transfer to a slow cooker.
2. Microwave onions, bacon, tomato paste, 1 tablespoon oregano, garlic, and ½ teaspoon salt in bowl, stirring occasionally, until onions are softened, about 5 minutes; transfer to a slow cooker. Stir in remaining beans, wine, parsnips, and carrots. Season pork with salt and pepper and stir into a slow cooker. Cover and cook until pork is tender, press the Slow Cook button, and cook on low for 6 to 8 hours or on high for 4 to 6 hours. (Press Slow Cook again to toggle between Low and High cooking temperatures.)
3. Preheat the oven to 450ºF (235ºC). Arrange bread in a single layer on a rimmed baking sheet and bake until browned and crisp, about 10 minutes, stirring halfway through baking. Toss croutons with oil and remaining 2 tablespoons oregano, and season with salt and pepper to taste. Set aside for serving.
4. Adjust consistency of filling as needed with hot water. Season with salt and pepper to taste. Top individual portions with croutons and drizzle with extra oil. Serve.

Baked Ziti with Sausage

Prep time: 15 minutes | **Cook time:** $2^1/_3$ to $3^1/_3$ hours | **Serves** 6 to 8

- 2 tablespoons extra-virgin olive oil
- 1 pound (454 g) hot or sweet Italian sausage, casings removed
- 1 onion, finely chopped
- Salt and pepper, to taste
- 3 garlic cloves, minced
- 2 teaspoons minced fresh oregano or ½ teaspoon dried
- 8 ounces (227 g) ziti
- 1 (28-ounce / 794-g) can crushed tomatoes
- 1 (15-ounce / 425-g) can tomato sauce
- 8 ounces (227 g) whole-milk ricotta cheese
- 4 ounces (113 g) Mozzarella cheese, shredded (1 cup)
- 2 tablespoons shredded fresh basil
- Vegetable oil spray

1. Line slow cooker with aluminum foil collar and lightly coat with vegetable oil spray. Heat oil in a Dutch oven over medium-high heat until just smoking. Cook sausage, breaking up pieces with wooden spoon, until well browned, 6 to 8 minutes. Stir in onion, ½ teaspoon salt, and ½ teaspoon pepper and cook until onion is softened and lightly browned, 5 to 7 minutes. Stir in garlic and oregano and cook until fragrant, about 1 minute.
2. Reduce heat to medium-low. Add ziti and cook, stirring constantly, until edges of pasta become translucent, about 4 minutes. Off heat, stir in tomatoes and tomato sauce, scraping up any browned bits. Transfer mixture to prepared slow cooker. Cover and cook until pasta is tender, press the Slow Cook button, and cook on high for 2 to 3 hours. (Press Slow Cook again to toggle between Low and High cooking temperatures.)
3. Discard foil collar. Dollop ricotta over ziti and sprinkle with Mozzarella. Cover and let sit until cheese is melted, about 20 minutes. Sprinkle with basil and serve.

CHAPTER 6 SOUPS, STEWS, AND CHILIES

Traditional Beef Vegetable Soup

Prep time: 25 minutes | **Cook time:** 6 to 9 hours | **Serves** 8 to 10

- 1 to 2 pounds (454 to 907 g) beef short ribs
- 2 quarts water
- 1 teaspoon salt
- 1 teaspoon celery salt
- 1 small onion, chopped
- 1 cup diced carrots
- ½ cup diced celery
- 2 cups diced potatoes
- 1 (1-pound / 454-g) can whole-kernel corn, undrained
- 1 (1-pound / 454-g) can diced tomatoes and juice

1. Combine meat, water, salt, celery salt, onion, carrots, and celery in a slow cooker.
2. Cover. Cook on low 4 to 6 hours.
3. Debone meat, cut into bite-sized pieces, and return to pot.
4. Add potatoes, corn, and tomatoes.
5. Cover and press the Slow Cook button, and cook on high for 2 to 3 hours. (Press Slow Cook again to toggle between Low and High cooking temperatures.)

Beef Alphabet Soup

Prep time: 10 minutes | **Cook time:** 6½ to 8½ hours | **Serves** 5 to 6

- ½ pound (227 g) beef stewing meat or round steak, cubed
- 1 (14½-ounce / 411-g) can stewed tomatoes
- 1 (8-ounce / 227-g) can tomato sauce
- 1 cup water
- 1 envelope dry onion soup mix
- 1 (10-ounce / 283-g) package frozen vegetables, partially thawed
- ½ cup alphabet noodles, uncooked

1. Combine meat, tomatoes, tomato sauce, water, and soup mix in a slow cooker.
2. Cover. Press the Slow Cook button, and cook on low for 6 to 8 hours. (Press Slow Cook again to toggle between Low and High cooking temperatures.) Turn to Highhigh.
3. Stir in vegetables and noodles. Add more water if mixture is too dry and thick.
4. Cover. Press the Slow Cook button, and cook on high for 30 minutes, or until vegetables are tender.

Creamy Carrot and Broccoli Soup

Prep time: 15 minutes | **Cook time:** 2½ to 3 hours | **Serves** 6 to 8

- 2 tablespoons unsalted butter
- 1 medium onion, finely chopped
- 3 medium carrots, cut into ½-inch dice
- 2 bunches broccoli (about 1½ pounds / 680 g), stems trimmed and cut into florets
- 1 teaspoon baking soda
- 3 cups chicken or vegetable broth
- Salt and freshly ground black pepper, to taste
- 1 cup heavy cream

1. Turn a slow cooker on high, add the butter to the insert, and cover until the butter is melted. Add the onion, carrots, and broccoli and toss the vegetables in the butter. Dissolve the baking soda in the broth and add to the vegetables.
2. Press the Slow Cook button, and cook on high for 2½ to 3 hours or on low for 5 to 6 hours. (Press Slow Cook again to toggle between Low and High cooking temperatures.)
3. Season with salt and pepper and stir in the cream. Turn off the slow cooker and let the soup rest for 15 minutes to come to serving temperature.

Pork and Black Bean Chili

Prep time: 10 minutes | **Cook time:** 6 to 8 hours | **Serves** 8

- 1 pound (454 g) pork tenderloin, cut into 1-inch chunks
- 1 (16-ounce / 454-g) jar thick chunky salsa
- 3 (15-ounce / 425-g) cans black beans, rinsed and drained
- ½ cup chicken broth
- 1 medium red bell pepper, chopped
- 1 medium onion, chopped
- 1 teaspoon ground cumin
- 2 to 3 teaspoons chili powder
- 1 to 1½ teaspoons dried oregano
- ¼ cup sour cream

4. Combine all ingredients except sour cream in a slow cooker.
5. Cover. Press the Slow Cook button, and cook on low for 6 to 8 hours, or until pork is tender. (Press Slow Cook again to toggle between Low and High cooking temperatures.)
6. Garnish individual servings with sour cream.

Beef Barley Soup with Veggies

Prep time: 10 minutes | **Cook time:** 5 to 7 hours | **Serves** 12

- 1 pound (454 g) lean stewing meat, cut into bite-sized pieces
- ½ cup onions, chopped
- ½ cup cut green beans, fresh or frozen
- ½ cup corn, fresh or frozen
- 4 cups fat-free, low-sodium beef broth
- 2 (14½-ounce / 411-g) cans low-sodium stewed tomatoes
- 1 (12-ounce / 340-g) can low-sodium V8 juice
- ⅔ cup pearl barley, uncooked
- 1 cup water

1. Combine all ingredients in a slow cooker.
2. Cover and press the Slow Cook button, and cook on high for 5 to 7 hours, until vegetables are cooked to your liking. (Press Slow Cook again to toggle between Low and High cooking temperatures.)

Mushroom and Bacon Soup

Prep time: 10 minutes | **Cook time:** 3 hours | **Serves** 8

- 8 strips bacon, cut into ½-inch dice
- 1 large onion, finely chopped
- 1 teaspoon dried sage leaves, crushed
- 1 pound (454 g) cremini mushrooms, sliced
- 1 pound (454 g) shiitake mushrooms, stems removed, and caps sliced
- 1 ounce (28 g) dried porcini mushrooms
- ¼ cup soy sauce
- 3 cups chicken broth
- 1 cup heavy cream
- ½ cup snipped fresh chives, for garnish

1. Sauté the bacon in a large skillet over medium heat until crisp and remove it from the pan to drain.
2. Add the onion and sage to the pan and sauté until the onion is softened. Add the cremini and shiitake mushrooms and toss until the mixture is combined.
3. Transfer the contents of the skillet to the insert of a slow cooker. Add the porcini mushrooms, soy sauce, broth, and bacon.
4. Cover and press the Slow Cook button, and cook on high for 3 hours or on low for 5 to 6 hours. (Press Slow Cook again to toggle between Low and High cooking temperatures.) At the end of the cooking time, add the cream and stir to combine.
5. Serve the soup garnished with the chives.

Red Pear and Pumpkin Soup

Prep time: 10 minutes | **Cook time:** 3 hours | **Serves** 8

- 4 tablespoons (½ stick) unsalted butter
- ½ cup finely chopped sweet onion
- ½ cup finely chopped celery
- ½ cup finely chopped carrot
- 2 medium red pears, peeled, cored, and finely chopped
- ½ teaspoon ground ginger
- 2 (15-ounce / 425-g) cans pumpkin purée
- 3 cups chicken broth
- Salt and freshly ground black pepper, to taste
- 1 cup heavy cream

1. Melt the butter in a medium skillet over medium-high heat. Add the onion, celery, carrot, pears, and ginger and sauté until the vegetables begin to soften, about 3 minutes. Transfer the contents of the skillet to the insert of a slow cooker.
2. Stir in the pumpkin and broth. Cover and press the Slow Cook button, and cook on high for 3 hours or on low for 5 to 6 hours. (Press Slow Cook again to toggle between Low and High cooking temperatures.)
3. Season with salt and pepper. Stir in the cream, cover, and leave on warm for 30 minutes before serving.

Vegetable Chili

Prep time: 20 minutes | **Cook time:** 6 to 8 hours | **Serves** 6

- 1 medium butternut squash, peeled and cubed
- 2 medium carrots, peeled and diced
- 1 medium onion, diced
- 3 teaspoons chili powder, or more to taste
- 2 (14-ounce / 397-g) cans diced tomatoes
- 1 (4-ounce / 113-g) can chopped mild green chilies
- 1 teaspoon salt (optional)
- 1 cup vegetable broth
- 2 (16-ounce / 454-g) cans black beans, drained and rinsed
- Sour cream (optional)

1. In a slow cooker, layer ingredients in order given—except sour cream.
2. Cover and press the Slow Cook button, and cook on low for 6 to 8 hours, or until vegetables are tender. (Press Slow Cook again to toggle between Low and High cooking temperatures.)
3. Stir before serving.
4. Top individual servings with dollops of sour cream.
5. Serve with crusty French bread.

Red Pear and Pumpkin Soup

Prep time: 10 minutes | **Cook time:** 3 hours | **Serves** 8

- 4 tablespoons (½ stick) unsalted butter
- ½ cup finely chopped sweet onion
- ½ cup finely chopped celery
- ½ cup finely chopped carrot
- 2 medium red pears, peeled, cored, and finely chopped
- ½ teaspoon ground ginger
- 2 (15-ounce / 425-g) cans pumpkin purée
- 3 cups chicken broth
- Salt and freshly ground black pepper, to taste
- 1 cup heavy cream

1. Melt the butter in a medium skillet over medium-high heat. Add the onion, celery, carrot, pears, and ginger and sauté until the vegetables begin to soften, about 3 minutes. Transfer the contents of the skillet to the insert of a slow cooker.
2. Stir in the pumpkin and broth. Cover and press the Slow Cook button, and cook on high for 3 hours or on low for 5 to 6 hours. (Press Slow Cook again to toggle between Low and High cooking temperatures.)
3. Season with salt and pepper. Stir in the cream, cover, and leave on warm for 30 minutes before serving.

Lamb and Carrot Stew

Prep time: 20 minutes | **Cook time:** 7 to 9 hours | **Serves** 6

- ½ cup all-purpose flour
- ½ teaspoon salt
- ¼ teaspoon pepper
- 1½ pounds (680 g) lamb stew meat, cubed
- 2 shallots, sliced
- 2 tablespoons olive oil
- ½ cup red wine
- 2 (14½-ounce / 411-g) cans beef broth
- 2 medium potatoes, cubed
- 1 large sweet potato, peeled and cubed
- 2 large carrots, cut into 1-inch pieces
- 2 medium parsnips, peeled and cubed
- 1 garlic clove, minced
- 1 tablespoon mint jelly
- 4 bacon strips, cooked and crumbled

1. In a large resealable plastic bag, combine the flour, salt and pepper. Add the meat, a few pieces at a time, and shake to coat. In a large skillet, brown meat and shallots in oil in batches.
2. Transfer to a slow cooker. Add wine to the skillet, stirring to loosen browned bits from pan. Bring to a boil. Reduce heat; simmer, uncovered, for 1-2 minutes. Add to a slow cooker.
3. Stir in the broth, potatoes, sweet potato, carrots, parsnips and garlic. Cover and press the Slow Cook button, and cook on low for 7 to 9 hours or until meat is tender. (Press Slow Cook again to toggle between Low and High cooking temperatures.)Stir in jelly; sprinkle with bacon.

Leek and Potato Soup

Prep time: 10 minutes | **Cook time:** 3 hours | **Serves** 8 to 10

- 4 tablespoons (½ stick) unsalted butter
- 4 leeks, finely chopped, using the white and a bit of the tender green parts
- 4 large russet potatoes, peeled and cut into 1-inch chunks
- 3 cups chicken broth
- Salt and freshly ground black pepper, to taste
- 1 cup heavy cream
- ½ cup snipped fresh chives, for garnish

1. Turn a slow cooker on high, add the butter to the insert, and cover until the butter is melted. Add the leeks and toss with the butter. Add the potatoes and broth. Cover the slow cooker and press the Slow Cook button, and cook on high for 3 hours or on low for 5 to 6 hours, until the potatoes are tender. (Press Slow Cook again to toggle between Low and High cooking temperatures.)
2. Purée the soup with an immersion blender, or mash with a potato masher. Season with salt and pepper. Stir in the cream and turn off the slow cooker. Cool the soup, then refrigerate until chilled.
3. Serve the soup in chilled bowls and garnish with the chives.

White Bean and Bacon Soup

Prep time: 15 minutes | **Cook time:** 8¼ to 9¼ hours | **Serves** 4 to 6

- 2 cups dried navy or great northern beans, picked over, soaked overnight, and drained
- 2 to 3 strips bacon, cooked, drained, and chopped
- 1 small yellow onion, finely chopped
- 1 rib celery, minced
- 1 small carrot, minced
- 1 bouquet garni: ½ teaspoon dried oregano, 3 sprigs fresh flat-leaf parsley, ½ fresh sage leaf, and 1 bay leaf, wrapped in cheesecloth and tied with kitchen twine
- 6 cups chicken broth or water
- Salt, to taste
- ¼ teaspoon freshly ground black pepper, or more to taste
- ½ cup heavy cream (optional)

1. Combine the beans, bacon, onion, celery, carrot, bouquet garni, and broth in the slow cooker. Cover and press the Slow Cook button, and cook on low for 8 to 9 hours. (Press Slow Cook again to toggle between Low and High cooking temperatures.)
2. Remove the bouquet garni and discard. Purée about one-third of the soup in a food processor or with a handheld immersion blender. Season with salt, then add the pepper and cream, if using, cover, and continue to cook on low 15 minutes longer. Ladle into soup bowls and serve hot.

CHAPTER 7 SIDE DISHES

Lemon Braised Artichokes

Prep time: 10 minutes | **Cook time:** 8 to 9 hours | **Serves** 4

- 4 artichokes
- ¼ cup lemon juice (2 lemons)
- 1 tablespoon extra-virgin olive oil
- 6 tablespoons unsalted butter
- 3 garlic cloves, minced
- ¼ teaspoon salt

1. Using chef's knife, cut off stems so artichokes sit upright, then trim off the top quarter of each artichoke. Using kitchen shears, trim off the top portion of outer leaves. Toss artichokes with 2 tablespoons lemon juice and oil in a bowl, then place right side up in a slow cooker. Add ½ cup water, cover, and press the Slow Cook button, and cook on low for 8 to 9 hours or on high for 5 to 6 hours, until outer leaves of artichokes pull away easily and tip of paring knife inserted into stem end meets no resistance. (Press Slow Cook again to toggle between Low and High cooking temperatures.)
2. Microwave remaining 2 tablespoons lemon juice, butter, garlic, and salt in the bowl until butter is melted, about 30 seconds. Whisk butter mixture to combine, then divide evenly among 4 serving bowls. Remove artichokes from the slow cooker, letting any excess cooking liquid drain back into insert, and place artichokes in bowls with butter. Serve.

Lemon and Parsley Fingerling Potatoes

Prep time: 10 minutes | **Cook time:** 5 to 6 hours | **Serves** 6

- 2 pounds (907 g) fingerling potatoes, unpeeled
- 2 tablespoons extra-virgin olive oil
- 2 scallions, white parts minced, green parts thinly sliced
- 3 garlic cloves, minced
- Salt and pepper, to taste
- 1 tablespoon chopped fresh parsley
- 1 teaspoon grated lemon zest plus 1 tablespoon juice

1. Combine potatoes, 1 tablespoon oil, scallion whites, garlic, 1 teaspoon salt, and ¼ teaspoon pepper in a slow cooker. Cover and press the Slow Cook button, and cook on low for 5 to 6 hours or on high for 3 to 4 hours, until potatoes are tender. (Press Slow Cook again to toggle between Low and High cooking temperatures.)
2. Stir in parsley, lemon zest and juice, scallion greens, and remaining 1 tablespoon oil. Season with salt and pepper to taste. Serve. (Potatoes can be held on warm or low setting for up to 2 hours.)

Creamy Mashed Cauliflower

Prep time: 10 minutes | **Cook time:** 7 to 8 hours | **Serves** 8 to 10

- 2 heads cauliflower (4 pounds / 1.8 kg), cored and cut into 2-inch florets
- ½ cup boiling water, plus extra as needed
- Salt and pepper, to taste
- ¼ cup heavy cream
- 3 tablespoons minced fresh chives

1. Combine cauliflower, boiling water, and 1½ teaspoons salt in a slow cooker. Press 16 by 12-inch sheet of parchment paper firmly onto cauliflower, folding down edges as needed. Cover and press the Slow Cook button, and cook on low for 7 to 8 hours or on high for 4 to 5 hours, until cauliflower is very tender. (Press Slow Cook again to toggle between Low and High cooking temperatures.)
2. Discard parchment. Mash cauliflower with potato masher until almost completely broken down. Stir in cream and chives and season with salt and pepper to taste. Serve. (Cauliflower can be held on warm or low setting for up to 2 hours; adjust consistency with extra hot water as needed before serving.)

Garlic Hash Browns

Prep time: 20 minutes | **Cook time:** 3 to 4 hours | **Serves** 12

- 1 large red onion, chopped
- 1 small sweet red pepper, chopped
- 1 small green pepper, chopped
- ¼ cup butter, cubed
- 1 tablespoon olive oil
- 4 garlic cloves, minced
- 1 (30-ounce / 850-g) package frozen shredded hash brown potatoes
- ½ teaspoon salt
- ½ teaspoon pepper
- 3 drops hot pepper sauce (optional)
- 2 teaspoons minced fresh parsley

1. In a large skillet, sauté onion and peppers in butter and oil until crisp-tender. Add garlic; cook 1 minute longer. Stir in the hash browns, salt, pepper and pepper sauce if desired.
2. Transfer to a slow cooker coated with cooking spray. Cover and press the Slow Cook button, and cook on low for 3 to 4 hours or until heated through. (Press Slow Cook again to toggle between Low and High cooking temperatures.)

Coconut-Pecan Sweet Potatoes

Prep time: 10 minutes | **Cook time:** 5 to 6 hours | **Serves** 6

- ¼ cup packed brown sugar
- 2 tablespoons flaked coconut
- 2 tablespoons chopped pecans, toasted
- 1 teaspoon vanilla extract
- ½ teaspoon salt
- ¼ teaspoon ground cinnamon
- 2 pounds (907 g) sweet potatoes, peeled and cut into ¾-inch cubes
- 1 tablespoon butter, melted
- ½ cup miniature marshmallows

1. In a small bowl, mix the first six ingredients. Place sweet potatoes in a slow cooker coated with cooking spray; sprinkle with brown sugar mixture. Drizzle with butter.
2. Cover and press the Slow Cook button, and cook on low for 5 to 6 hours or until the sweet potatoes are tender. (Press Slow Cook again to toggle between Low and High cooking temperatures.) Turn off the slow cooker. Sprinkle the marshmallows over potatoes; let stand, covered, 5 minutes before serving.

Roasted Beets with Oranges and Walnuts

Prep time: 10 minutes | **Cook time:** 6 to 7 hours | **Serves** 4 to 6

- 1½ pounds (680 g) beets, trimmed
- 2 oranges
- ¼ cup white wine vinegar
- 2 tablespoons extra-virgin olive oil
- 1 tablespoon honey
- Salt and pepper, to taste
- ¼ cup toasted and chopped walnuts
- 2 tablespoons minced fresh chives

1. Wrap beets individually in aluminum foil and place in a slow cooker. Add ½ cup water, cover, and press the Slow Cook button, and cook on low for 6 to 7 hours or on high for 4 to 5 hours. (Press Slow Cook again to toggle between Low and High cooking temperatures.)
2. Transfer beets to cutting board and carefully remove foil (watch for steam). When beets are cool enough to handle, rub off skins with paper towels and cut into ½-inch-thick wedges.
3. Cut away peel and pith from oranges. Quarter oranges, then slice crosswise into ½-inch-thick pieces. Whisk vinegar, oil, and honey together in large bowl. Add beets and orange pieces, along with any accumulated juices, and toss to coat. Season with salt and pepper to taste. Sprinkle with walnuts and chives. Serve.

Cheesy Red Potatoes

Prep time: 15 minutes | **Cook time:** 5 to 6 hours | **Serves** 8

- 7 cups cubed uncooked red potatoes
- 1 cup (8 ounces / 227 g) 4% cottage cheese
- ½ cup sour cream
- ½ cup cubed process cheese (Velveeta)
- 1 tablespoon dried minced onion
- 2 garlic cloves, minced
- ½ teaspoon salt
- Paprika and minced chives (optional)

1. Place the potatoes in a slow cooker. In a blender, purée cottage cheese and sour cream until smooth. Transfer to a large bowl; stir in the process cheese, onion, garlic and salt. Pour over potatoes and mix well.
2. Cover and press the Slow Cook button, and cook on low for 5 to 6 hours or until potatoes are tender. (Press Slow Cook again to toggle between Low and High cooking temperatures.) Stir well before serving. Garnish with paprika and chives if desired.

Marmalade Glazed Carrots

Prep time: 10 minutes | **Cook time:** 5 to 6 hours | **Serves** 6 to 8

- 3 pounds (1.4 kg) carrots, peeled and sliced ¼ inch thick on bias
- 1 tablespoon sugar
- Salt and pepper, to taste
- ½ cup orange marmalade
- 2 tablespoons unsalted butter, softened

1. Combine carrots, ¾ cup water, sugar, and ¼ teaspoon salt in a slow cooker. Cover and press the Slow Cook button, and cook on low for 5 to 6 hours or on high for 3 to 4 hours, until carrots are tender. (Press Slow Cook again to toggle between Low and High cooking temperatures.)
2. Drain carrots and return to now-empty slow cooker. Stir in marmalade and butter. Season with salt and pepper to taste. Serve. (Carrots can be held on warm or low setting for up to 2 hours.)

Thyme Garlic Tomatoes

Prep time: 15 minutes | **Cook time:** 5 to 6 hours | **Serves** 4 to 6

- 6 ripe tomatoes, cored and halved crosswise
- ½ cup extra-virgin olive oil
- 6 garlic cloves, peeled and smashed
- 2 teaspoons minced fresh thyme or ¾ teaspoon dried
- Salt and pepper, to taste

1. Combine tomatoes, oil, garlic, thyme, ¾ teaspoon salt, and ¼ teaspoon pepper in a slow cooker. Cover and press the Slow Cook button, and cook on low for 5 to 6 hours or on high for 3 to 4 hours, until tomatoes are tender and slightly shriveled around edges. (Press Slow Cook again to toggle between Low and High cooking temperatures.)
2. Let tomatoes cool in oil for at least 15 minutes or up to 4 hours. Season with salt and pepper to taste. Serve.

Buttered Parsley Red Potatoes

Prep time: 10 minutes | **Cook time:** 2½ to 3 hours | **Serves** 6

- 1½ pounds (680 g) medium red potatoes
- ¼ cup water
- ¼ cup butter, melted
- 3 tablespoons minced fresh parsley
- 1 tablespoon lemon juice
- 1 tablespoon minced chives
- Salt and pepper, to taste

1. Cut a strip of peel from around the middle of each potato. Place potatoes and water in a slow cooker. Cover and press the Slow Cook button, and cook on high for 2½ to 3 hours or until tender (do not overcook); drain. (Press Slow Cook again to toggle between Low and High cooking temperatures.)
2. In a small bowl, combine the butter, parsley, lemon juice and chives. Pour over the potatoes and toss to coat. Season with salt and pepper.

Spinach and Cheese Casserole

Prep time: 10 minutes | **Cook time:** 2½ hours | **Serves** 8

- 2 (10-ounce / 283-g) packages frozen chopped spinach, thawed and well drained
- 2 cups 4% cottage cheese
- 1 cup cubed process cheese (Velveeta)
- ¾ cup egg substitute
- 2 tablespoons butter, cubed
- ¼ cup all-purpose flour
- ½ teaspoon salt

1. In a slow cooker, combine all ingredients. Cover and press the Slow Cook button, and cook on low for 2½ hours or until cheese is melted. (Press Slow Cook again to toggle between Low and High cooking temperatures.).

Butter Mushrooms

Prep time: 10 minutes | **Cook time:** 4 to 5 hours | **Serves** 6

- 1 pound (454 g) medium fresh mushrooms
- 1 large onion, sliced
- ½ cup butter, melted
- 1 envelope Italian salad dressing mix

1. In a slow cooker, layer mushrooms and onion. Combine butter and salad dressing mix; pour over vegetables. Cover and press the Slow Cook button, and cook on low for 4 to 5 hours or until vegetables are tender. (Press Slow Cook again to toggle between Low and High cooking temperatures.) Serve with a slotted spoon.

Honey Glazed Peas and Carrots

Prep time: 15 minutes | **Cook time:** 5¼ hours | **Serves** 12

- 1 pound (454 g) carrots, sliced
- 1 large onion, chopped
- ¼ cup water
- ¼ cup butter, cubed
- ¼ cup honey
- 4 garlic cloves, minced
- 1 teaspoon salt
- 1 teaspoon dried marjoram
- ⅛ teaspoon white pepper
- 1 (16-ounce / 454-g) package frozen peas

1. In a slow cooker, combine the first nine ingredients. Cook, covered, on low 5 hours. Stir in the peas. Cover and press the Slow Cook button, and cook on high for 15 to 25 minutes or until the vegetables are tender. (Press Slow Cook again to toggle between Low and High cooking temperatures.)

CHAPTER 8 VEGETARIAN MAINS

Red Tofu Curry and Green Beans

Prep time: 15 minutes | **Cook time:** 6 hours | **Serves** 2

- 1 teaspoon extra-virgin olive oil
- 16 ounces (454 g) firm tofu, drained and cut into 1-inch pieces
- 2 cups chopped green beans
- ½ red onion, halved and thinly sliced
- 1 plum tomato, diced
- 1 teaspoon minced fresh ginger
- 1 teaspoon minced garlic
- 2 teaspoons Thai red curry paste
- 1 cup coconut milk
- 1 cup low-sodium vegetable broth

1. Grease the inside of the slow cooker with the olive oil.
2. Put all the ingredients into the slow cooker and stir gently.
3. Cover and press the Slow Cook button, and cook on low for 6 hours. (Press Slow Cook again to toggle between Low and High cooking temperatures.)

Curried Sweet Potatoes and Broccoli

Prep time: 10 minutes | **Cook time:** 6 to 8 hours | **Serves** 2

- 2 medium sweet potatoes, cut into 1-inch pieces
- 1 cup broccoli florets
- ½ cup diced onions
- 1 cup light coconut milk
- 1 teaspoon minced fresh ginger
- 1 teaspoon minced garlic
- Pinch red pepper flakes
- 1 tablespoon curry powder
- 1 teaspoon garam masala
- ¼ cup toasted cashews

1. Put the sweet potatoes, broccoli, and onions into the slow cooker.
2. In a small bowl, whisk together the coconut milk, ginger, garlic, red pepper flakes, curry powder, and garam masala. Pour this mixture over the vegetables.
3. Cover and press the Slow Cook button, and cook on low for 6 to 8 hours, , until the vegetables are very tender but not falling apart. (Press Slow Cook again to toggle between Low and High cooking temperatures.)
4. Just before serving, add the cashews and stir thoroughly.

Red Beans and Rice with Okra

Prep time: 15 minutes | **Cook time:** 8 to 9 hours | **Serves** 4 to 6

- 2 tablespoons Cajun seasoning
- 2 tablespoons extra-virgin olive oil
- 3 garlic cloves, minced
- 4 cups vegetable broth
- 8 ounces (227 g) dried small red beans, picked over and rinsed
- 1 green bell pepper, stemmed, deseeded, and cut into ½-inch pieces
- 1½ cups instant white rice
- 2 cups frozen cut okra, thawed
- 2 tomatoes, cored and cut into ½-inch pieces
- 4 scallions, thinly sliced
- Salt and pepper, to taste

1. Microwave Cajun seasoning, oil, and garlic in bowl until fragrant, about 1 minute; transfer to a slow cooker. Stir in broth, beans, and bell pepper. Cover and press the Slow Cook button, and cook on high for 8 to 9 hours, until beans are tender. (Press Slow Cook again to toggle between Low and High cooking temperatures.)
2. Stir in rice, cover, and press the Slow Cook button, and cook on high for 20 to 30 minutes, until rice is tender. (Press Slow Cook again to toggle between Low and High cooking temperatures.) Stir in okra and let sit until heated through, about 5 minutes. Stir in tomatoes and scallions, and season with salt and pepper to taste. Serve.

Summer Squash, Kale, and Quinoa Stew

Prep time: 10 minutes | **Cook time:** 4 hours | **Serves** 2

- ½ cup quinoa
- ½ cup canned chickpeas, drained and rinsed
- 1 cup diced summer squash
- 4 cups fresh kale
- 1 cup canned plum tomatoes, roughly chopped
- 2 cups low-sodium vegetable broth
- 1 tablespoon Italian herb blend
- ⅛ teaspoon sea salt

1. Put all the ingredients into the slow cooker, stirring to mix them together thoroughly.
2. Cover and press the Slow Cook button, and cook on low for 4 hours. (Press Slow Cook again to toggle between Low and High cooking temperatures.)

Rosemary Cauliflower and Lentils

Prep time: 10 minutes | **Cook time:** 8 hours | **Serves** 2

- 1 cup cauliflower florets
- 1 cup lentils
- 1 tablespoon fresh rosemary
- 1 tablespoon roasted garlic
- Zest of 1 lemon
- 1 tablespoon extra-virgin olive oil
- ⅛ teaspoon sea salt
- Freshly ground black pepper, to taste
- 3 cups low-sodium vegetable broth
- Juice of 1 lemon
- ¼ cup roughly chopped fresh parsley

1. Put the cauliflower, lentils, rosemary, garlic, lemon zest, and olive oil in the slow cooker. Season with the salt and black pepper.
2. Pour the vegetable broth over the cauliflower and lentils. Cover and press the Slow Cook button, and cook on low for 8 hours. (Press Slow Cook again to toggle between Low and High cooking temperatures.)
3. Just before serving, drizzle the cauliflower and lentils with the lemon juice and sprinkle the parsley over the top.

Smoky Mixed Bean Chili

Prep time: 10 minutes | **Cook time:** 6 to 8 hours | **Serves** 2

- 1 (16-ounce / 454-g) can mixed beans, drained and rinsed
- 1 cup frozen roasted corn kernels, thawed
- 1 cup canned fire-roasted diced tomatoes, undrained
- ½ cup diced onion
- 2 garlic cloves, minced
- 1 teaspoon ground cumin
- 1 teaspoon smoked paprika
- 1 teaspoon dried oregano
- ⅛ teaspoon sea salt

1. Put all the ingredients in the slow cooker. Give them a quick stir to combine.
2. Cover and press the Slow Cook button, and cook on low for 6 to 8 hours. (Press Slow Cook again to toggle between Low and High cooking temperatures.)

Tempeh and Corn Stuffed Bell Peppers

Prep time: 10 minutes | **Cook time:** 6 to 8 hours | **Serves** 2

- 1 teaspoon extra-virgin olive oil
- 8 ounces (227 g) tempeh, crumbled
- 1 cup frozen corn kernels, thawed
- ¼ cup minced onions
- 1 teaspoon minced garlic
- 1 teaspoon ground cumin
- 1 teaspoon smoked paprika
- 2 tablespoons Pepper Jack cheese
- ⅛ teaspoon sea salt
- 4 narrow red bell peppers

1. Grease the inside of the slow cooker with the olive oil.
2. In a medium bowl, combine the tempeh, corn, onions, garlic, cumin, paprika, cheese, and salt.
3. Cut the tops off each of the peppers and set the tops aside. Scoop out and discard the seeds and membranes from inside each pepper. Divide the tempeh filling among the peppers. Return the tops to each of the peppers.
4. Nestle the peppers into the slow cooker.
5. Cover and press the Slow Cook button, and cook on low for 6 to 8 hours, until the peppers are very tender. (Press Slow Cook again to toggle between Low and High cooking temperatures.)

Vegetarian Bean Cassoulet

Prep time: 10 minutes | **Cook time:** 6 to 8 hours | **Serves** 2

- 1 teaspoon extra-virgin olive oil
- 2 (15-ounce / 425-g) cans navy beans, drained and rinsed
- 16 ounces (454 g) vegan sausage, cut into 1-inch pieces
- 1 cup minced onion
- ¼ cup minced celery
- 1 tablespoon minced garlic
- 1 teaspoon minced fresh sage
- 1 cup low-sodium vegetable broth

1. Grease the inside of the slow cooker with the olive oil.
2. Put the beans, sausage, onion, celery, garlic, and sage in the slow cooker. Stir to mix thoroughly. Pour in the vegetable broth.
3. Cover and press the Slow Cook button, and cook on low for 6 to 8 hours, , until the beans are very tender but not falling apart. (Press Slow Cook again to toggle between Low and High cooking temperatures.)

Beet and Wheat Berry Salad

Prep time: 10 minutes | **Cook time:** 6 to 8 hours | **Serves** 4 to 6

- 1 cup wheat berries
- 2 garlic cloves, minced
- 2 teaspoons minced fresh thyme or ½ teaspoon dried
- Salt and pepper, to taste
- 1 pound (454 g) beets, trimmed
- 1 Granny Smith apple, peeled, cored, halved, and sliced ¼ inch thick
- 4 ounces (113 g) baby arugula
- 3 tablespoons extra-virgin olive oil
- 3 tablespoons red wine vinegar
- Pinch sugar
- 4 ounces (113 g) goat cheese, crumbled (1 cup)

1. Combine 5 cups water, wheat berries, garlic, thyme, and ½ teaspoon salt in a slow cooker. Wrap beets individually in aluminum foil and place in a slow cooker. Cover and press the Slow Cook button, and cook on low for 6 to 8 hours or on high for 4 to 5 hours, until wheat berries and beets are tender. (Press Slow Cook again to toggle between Low and High cooking temperatures.)
2. Transfer beets to cutting board, open foil, and let sit until cool enough to handle. Rub off beet skins with paper towels and cut beets into ½-inch-thick wedges.
3. Drain wheat berries, transfer to a large serving bowl, and let cool slightly. Add beets, apple, arugula, oil, vinegar, ½ teaspoon salt, pinch pepper, and sugar and toss to combine. Season with salt and pepper to taste. Sprinkle with goat cheese and serve.

CHAPTER 9 POULTRY

Roasted Chicken and Vegetables

Prep time: 15 minutes | **Cook time:** 8 to 10 hours | **Serves** 6

- 2 carrots, sliced
- 2 onions, sliced
- 2 celery ribs, cut into 1-inch pieces
- 3 pounds (1.4 kg) chicken, whole or cut up
- 2 teaspoons salt
- ½ teaspoon dried coarse black pepper
- 1 teaspoon dried basil
- ½ cup water, chicken broth, or white cooking wine

1. Place vegetables in bottom of the slow cooker. Place chicken on top of vegetables. Add seasonings and water.
2. Cover. Press the Slow Cook button, and cook on low for 8 to 10 hours or on high for 3½ to 5 hours (use 1 cup liquid if cooking on high). (Press Slow Cook again to toggle between Low and High cooking temperatures.) Serve.

Asian Ginger Chicken

Prep time: 15 minutes | **Cook time:** 3 to 5 hours | **Serves** 6

- 6 chicken breast halves, uncooked, cut up
- 1 cup diced carrots
- ½ cup minced onion
- ½ cup low-sodium soy sauce
- ¼ cup rice vinegar
- ¼ cup sesame seeds
- 1 tablespoon ground ginger, or ¼ cup grated ginger
- ¾ teaspoon salt
- 1 teaspoon sesame oil
- 2 cups broccoli florets
- 1 cup cauliflower florets

1. Combine all ingredients except broccoli and cauliflower in a slow cooker.
2. Cover. Press the Slow Cook button, and cook on low for 3 to 5 hours. (Press Slow Cook again to toggle between Low and High cooking temperatures.) Stir in broccoli and cauliflower and cook an additional hour.
3. Serve over brown rice.

Basil Chicken

Prep time: 5 minutes | **Cook time:** 5 to 6 hours | **Serves** 6

- 6 boneless, skinless chicken breast halves
- 2 (10¾-ounce / 305-g) cans broccoli cheese soup
- 2 cups milk
- 1 small onion, chopped
- ½ to 1 teaspoon salt
- ½ to 1 teaspoon dried basil
- ⅛ teaspoon pepper

1. Place chicken pieces in a slow cooker.
2. Combine remaining ingredients. Pour over chicken.
3. Cover. Press the Slow Cook button, and cook on high for 1 hour. Turn the cooker to cook on low for 5 to 6 hours. (Press Slow Cook again to toggle between Low and High cooking temperatures.)
4. Serve over noodles.

Thai Sesame Chicken Thighs

Prep time: 20 minutes | **Cook time:** 5 to 6 hours | **Serves** 8

- 8 bone-in chicken thighs (about 3 pounds / 1.4 kg), skin removed
- ½ cup salsa
- ¼ cup creamy peanut butter
- 2 tablespoons lemon juice
- 2 tablespoons reduced-sodium soy sauce
- 1 tablespoon chopped deseeded jalapeño pepper
- 2 teaspoons Thai chili sauce
- 1 garlic clove, minced
- 1 teaspoon minced fresh ginger
- 2 green onions, sliced
- 2 tablespoons sesame seeds, toasted
- Hot cooked basmati rice (optional)

1. Place chicken in a slow cooker. In a small bowl, combine the salsa, peanut butter, lemon juice, soy sauce, jalapeño, Thai chili sauce, garlic and ginger; pour over chicken.
2. Cover and press the Slow Cook button, and cook on low for 5 to 6 hours or until chicken is tender. (Press Slow Cook again to toggle between Low and High cooking temperatures.) Sprinkle with green onions and sesame seeds. Serve with rice if desired.

Honey Butter Baked Chicken

Prep time: 15 minutes | **Cook time:** 3 hours | **Serves** 4

- 4 skinless, bone-in chicken breast halves
- 2 tablespoons butter, melted
- 2 tablespoons honey
- 2 teaspoons prepared mustard
- 2 teaspoons curry powder
- Salt and pepper, to taste (optional)

1. Spray slow cooker with nonstick cooking spray and add chicken
2. Mix butter, honey, mustard, and curry powder together in a small bowl. Pour sauce over chicken.
3. Cover and press the Slow Cook button, and cook on low for 5 to 6 hours or on high for 3 hours. (Press Slow Cook again to toggle between Low and High cooking temperatures.)

Creamy Lemon Garlic Chicken

Prep time: 15 minutes | **Cook time:** 3 to 4 hours | **Serves** 6

- 1 cup vegetable broth
- 1½ teaspoons grated lemon peel
- 3 tablespoons lemon juice
- 2 tablespoons capers, drained
- 3 garlic cloves, minced
- ½ teaspoon pepper
- 6 boneless skinless chicken breast halves (6 ounces / 170 g each)
- 2 tablespoons butter
- 2 tablespoons all-purpose flour
- ½ cup heavy whipping cream
- Hot cooked rice

1. In a small bowl, combine the first six ingredients. Place chicken in a slow cooker; pour broth mixture over chicken. Cover and press the Slow Cook button, and cook on low for 3 to 5 hours or until chicken is tender. (Press Slow Cook again to toggle between Low and High cooking temperatures.)
2. Remove chicken from slow cooker; keep warm. In a large saucepan, melt butter over medium heat. Stir in flour until smooth; gradually whisk in cooking juices. Bring to a boil, stirring constantly; cook and stir 1-2 minutes or until thickened. Remove from heat and stir in cream. Serve chicken and rice with sauce.

Picnic Chicken

Prep time: 5 minutes | **Cook time:** 6 to 7 hours | **Serves** 4

- 2 pounds (907 g) or 4 large chicken thighs
- ¼ cup dill pickle relish
- ¼ cup Dijon mustard
- ¼ cup mayonnaise
- ½ cup chicken broth

1. Rinse chicken well. Pat dry. Place in a slow cooker with the skin side up.
2. In a mixing bowl, stir together the relish, mustard, and mayonnaise. When well blended, stir in chicken broth. Mix well.
3. Pour sauce over chicken.
4. Cover cooker and press the Slow Cook button, and cook on low for 6 to 7 hours, or until chicken is tender but not dry or mushy. (Press Slow Cook again to toggle between Low and High cooking temperatures.)

Salsa Curry Chicken

Prep time: 15 minutes | **Cook time:** 3 to 4½ hours | **Serves** 10

- 10 skinless, bone-in chicken breast halves, divided
- 1 (16-ounce / 454-g) jar salsa, your choice of heat
- 1 medium onion, chopped
- 2 tablespoons curry powder
- 1 cup sour cream

1. Place half the chicken in the slow cooker.
2. Combine salsa, onion, and curry powder in a medium-sized bowl. Pour half the sauce over the meat in the cooker.
3. Repeat Steps 1 and 2.
4. Cover and press the Slow Cook button, and cook on high for 3 hours. Or cook on high for 1½ hours and then turn cooker to low and cook 3 more hours. (Press Slow Cook again to toggle between Low and High cooking temperatures.).
5. Remove chicken to serving platter and cover to keep warm.
6. Add sour cream to slow cooker and stir into salsa until well blended. Serve over the chicken.

Garlic and Citrus Chicken

Prep time: 15 minutes | **Cook time:** 5 to 6 hours | **Serves** 6

- 6 skinless, bone-in chicken breast halves
- 1½ teaspoons dry thyme
- 6 cloves garlic, minced
- 1 cup orange juice concentrate
- 2 tablespoons balsamic vinegar

1. Rub thyme and garlic over chicken. (Reserve any leftover thyme and garlic.) Place chicken in a slow cooker.
2. Mix orange juice concentrate and vinegar together in a small bowl. Stir in reserved thyme and garlic. Spoon over chicken.
3. Cover and press the Slow Cook button, and cook on low for 5 to 6 hours or on high for 2½ to 3 hours, until chicken is tender but not dry. (Press Slow Cook again to toggle between Low and High cooking temperatures.)

Stuffed Chicken with Bacon and Feta

Prep time: 10 minutes | **Cook time:** 1½ to 3 hours | **Serves** 4

- ¼ cup crumbled cooked bacon
- ¼ cup crumbled feta cheese
- 4 boneless, skinless chicken breast halves
- 2 (14½-ounce / 411-g) cans diced tomatoes
- 1 tablespoon dried basil

1. In a small bowl, mix bacon and cheese together lightly.
2. Cut a pocket in the thicker side of each chicken breast. Fill each with ¼ of the bacon and cheese. Pinch shut and secure with toothpicks.
3. Place chicken in a slow cooker. Top with tomatoes and sprinkle with basil.
4. Cover and press the Slow Cook button, and cook on high for 1½ to 3 hours, or until chicken is tender, but not dry or mushy. (Press Slow Cook again to toggle between Low and High cooking temperatures.)

Lemon Pepper Chicken

Prep time: 5 minutes | **Cook time:** 6 to 8 hours | **Serves** 4

- 1 onion, chopped
- 1 pound (454 g) boneless, skinless chicken thighs
- 1 teaspoon lemon pepper
- ½ teaspoon dried oregano
- ½ cup plain yogurt

1. Combine first 3 ingredients in a slow cooker. Cover and press the Slow Cook button, and cook on low for 6 to 8 hours, or until chicken is tender. (Press Slow Cook again to toggle between Low and High cooking temperatures.)
2. Just before serving, remove chicken and shred with two forks.
3. Add shredded chicken back into a slow cooker and stir in oregano and yogurt.
4. Serve as a filling for pita bread.

Chicken and Potato Bake

Prep time: 15 minutes | **Cook time:** 4½ to 5½ hours | **Serves** 6 to 8

- ¼ cup chopped green peppers
- ½ cup chopped onions
- 1½ cups diced Velveeta cheese
- 7 to 8 medium potatoes, sliced
- Salt, to taste
- 1 (10¾-ounce / 305-g) can cream of celery soup
- 1 cup milk
- 3 to 4 whole boneless, skinless chicken breasts

1. Place layers of green peppers, onions, cheese, and potatoes and a sprinkling of salt in a slow cooker.
2. Sprinkle salt over chicken breasts and lay on top of potatoes.
3. Combine soup and milk and pour into a slow cooker, pushing meat down into liquid.
4. Cover. Press the Slow Cook button, and cook on high for 1½ hours. Turn the cooker to cook on low for 3 to 4 hours (Press Slow Cook again to toggle between Low and High cooking temperatures.) Test that potatoes are soft. If not, continue cooking on low another hour and test again, continuing to cook until potatoes are finished.

CHAPTER 10 MEAT

Basil Beef Steak with Mushrooms

Prep time: 15 minutes | **Cook time:** 6 to 8 hours | **Serves** 4

- 1¼ pounds (567 g) boneless beef shoulder top blade or flat iron steaks
- ½ pound (227 g) whole fresh mushrooms, quartered
- 1 medium sweet yellow pepper, julienned
- 1 (14½-ounce / 411-g) can stewed tomatoes, undrained
- 1 (8-ounce / 227-g) can tomato sauce
- 1 envelope onion soup mix
- 2 tablespoons minced fresh basil
- Hot cooked rice, for serving

1. Place steaks in a slow cooker. Add mushrooms and pepper. In a bowl, mix tomatoes, tomato sauce, soup mix and basil; pour over top.
2. Cover and press the Slow Cook button, and cook on low for 6 to 8 hours or until beef and vegetables are tender. (Press Slow Cook again to toggle between Low and High cooking temperatures.) Serve with rice.

Sausage and Peppers in Wine

Prep time: 15 minutes | **Cook time:** 6 to 8 hours | **Serves** 4 to 6

- 3 large assorted colored bell peppers, such as red, yellow, and orange, deseeded and cut into chunks
- 1 large yellow onion, cut into wedges
- 3 cloves garlic, peeled
- Salt and freshly ground black pepper, to taste
- 1 tablespoon minced fresh thyme
- 2 tablespoons olive oil
- 2 pounds (907 g) assorted sausages, such as hot and sweet Italian and chicken basil
- ⅓ cup dry red wine

1. Put the peppers in the slow cooker. Add the onion and garlic and toss to combine. Sprinkle with a small amount of salt and pepper and all the thyme.
2. In a large skillet, heat the olive oil over medium-high heat and brown the sausages all over, 3 to 5 minutes, pricking them with a fork. Place them on top of the vegetables in the cooker. Add the wine to the skillet and bring to a boil, scraping up any browned bits stuck to the pan. Pour into the cooker. Cover and press the Slow Cook button, and cook on low for 6 to 8 hours. (Press Slow Cook again to toggle between Low and High cooking temperatures.) Serve the sausage and peppers hot.

Cheesy Beef-Stuffed Peppers

Prep time: 15 minutes | **Cook time:** 5 to 6 hours | **Serves** 4

- 4 medium green or sweet red peppers
- 1 pound (454 g) ground beef
- 1 (8.8-ounce / 249-g) package ready-to-serve Spanish rice
- 2 cups shredded Colby-Monterey Jack cheese, divided
- 1½ cups salsa
- 1 tablespoon hot pepper sauce
- 1 cup water
- 2 tablespoons minced fresh cilantro

1. Cut tops off peppers and remove seeds; set aside. In a large skillet, cook beef over medium heat until no longer pink; drain.
2. Stir in the rice, 1½ cups cheese, salsa and pepper sauce. Spoon into peppers. Transfer to a slow cooker. Pour water around peppers.
3. Cover and press the Slow Cook button, and cook on low for 5 to 6 hours or until peppers are tender and filling is heated through. (Press Slow Cook again to toggle between Low and High cooking temperatures.) Top with remaining cheese; sprinkle with cilantro.

Garlicky Beef with Sesame

Prep time: 15 minutes | **Cook time:** 5 to 7 hours | **Serves** 6

- 6 green onions, sliced
- ½ cup sugar
- ½ cup water
- ½ cup reduced-sodium soy sauce
- ¼ cup sesame oil
- 3 tablespoons toasted sesame seeds
- 2 tablespoons all-purpose flour
- 4 garlic cloves, minced
- 1 beef sirloin tip roast (3 pounds / 1.4 kg), thinly sliced
- Additional sliced green onions and toasted sesame seeds
- Hot cooked rice, for serving

1. In a large resealable plastic bag, mix the first eight ingredients. Add beef; seal bag and turn to coat. Refrigerate 8 hours or overnight.
2. Pour beef and marinade into a slow cooker. Cover and press the Slow Cook button, and cook on low for 5 to 7 hours or until meat is tender. (Press Slow Cook again to toggle between Low and High cooking temperatures.)
3. Using a slotted spoon, remove beef to a serving platter; sprinkle with additional green onions and sesame seeds. Serve with rice.

BBQ Beef Sandwiches

Prep time: 5 minutes | **Cook time:** 8 to 10 hours | **Serves** 8

- 1 boneless beef chuck roast (3 pounds / 1.4 kg)
- 1 envelope chili seasoning
- ½ cup barbecue sauce
- 8 onion rolls, split
- 8 slices Cheddar cheese

1. Cut roast in half; place in a slow cooker. Sprinkle with chili seasoning. Pour barbecue sauce over top. Cover and press the Slow Cook button, and cook on low for 8 to 10 hours or until meat is tender. (Press Slow Cook again to toggle between Low and High cooking temperatures.)
2. Remove roast; cool slightly. Shred meat with two forks. Skim fat from cooking juices. Return meat to slow cooker; heat through. Using a slotted spoon, place ½ cup meat mixture on each roll bottom; top with cheese. Replace tops.

Pork Tenderloin with Mango Sauce

Prep time: 20 minutes | **Cook time:** 3 hours | **Serves** 6

- 4 tablespoons (½ stick) unsalted butter, melted
- 2 large mangoes, peeled, pitted, and coarsely chopped
- 2 navel oranges, peeled and sectioned
- 2 tablespoons soy sauce
- ½ cup dark rum
- ½ cup beef broth
- 2 (1-pound / 454-g) pork tenderloins
- 2 tablespoons Jamaican jerk seasoning
- 6 green onions, finely chopped, using the white and tender green parts for garnish

1. Stir the butter, mangoes, oranges, soy sauce, rum, and broth together in the insert of a slow cooker. Remove the silver skin from the outside of the pork with a boning knife and discard.
2. Rub the jerk seasoning on the pork and arrange it in the slow cooker. Cover and press the Slow Cook button, and cook on high for 3 hours, until the pork is tender and cooked through. (The pork should register 175ºF (79ºC) on an instant-read thermometer.) (Press Slow Cook again to toggle between Low and High cooking temperatures.)
3. Remove the pork from the sauce, cover with aluminum foil, and allow to rest for 20 minutes. Skim off any fat from the top of the sauce.
4. Slice the meat and garnish with the green onions. Serve the sauce on the side.

Pork Chili Verde

Prep time: 10 minutes | **Cook time:** 5 to 6 hours | **Serves** 12

- 1 boneless pork shoulder roast (4 to 5 pounds / 1.8 to 2.3 kg), cut into 1-inch pieces
- 3 (10-ounce / 283-g) cans green enchilada sauce
- 1 cup salsa verde
- 1 (4-ounce / 113-g) can chopped green chilies
- ½ teaspoon salt
- Hot cooked rice, for serving
- Sour cream (optional)

1. In a slow cooker, combine pork, enchilada sauce, salsa verde, green chilies and salt. Cover and press the Slow Cook button, and cook on low for 5 to 6 hours or until pork is tender. (Press Slow Cook again to toggle between Low and High cooking temperatures.) Serve with rice. If desired, top with sour cream.

Teriyaki Pork Tenderloin

Prep time: 5 minutes | **Cook time:** 3 hours | **Serves** 6

- 2 tablespoons vegetable oil
- 2 cloves garlic, minced
- 1 teaspoon grated fresh ginger
- 1 cup soy sauce
- ¼ cup rice vinegar
- 3 tablespoons light brown sugar
- 2 (1-pound / 454-g) pork tenderloins

1. Whisk the oil, garlic, ginger, soy sauce, vinegar, and sugar together in a bowl until blended. Remove the silver skin from the outside of the pork with a boning knife and discard.
2. Place the tenderloins in a 1-gallon zipper-top plastic bag or 13-by-9-inch baking dish. Pour the marinade over the tenderloins and seal the bag or cover the dish with plastic wrap.
3. Marinate for at least 4 hours or overnight, turning the meat once or twice during that time. Place the marinade and pork in the insert of a slow cooker. Cover and press the Slow Cook button, and cook on high for 3 hours. (Press Slow Cook again to toggle between Low and High cooking temperatures.)
4. Remove the meat from the sauce, cover loosely with aluminum foil, and allow the meat to rest for about 10 minutes. Skim off any fat from the top of the sauce.
5. Cut the meat diagonally in ½-inch-thick slices. Nap each serving of pork with some of the sauce.

Pork Ribs with Peach Sauce

Prep time: 20 minutes | **Cook time:** 5½ to 6½ hours | **Serves** 4

- 2 pounds (907 g) boneless country-style pork ribs
- 2 tablespoons taco seasoning
- ½ cup mild salsa
- ¼ cup peach pre**Serves**
- ¼ cup barbecue sauce
- 2 cups chopped fresh peeled peaches or frozen unsweetened sliced peaches, thawed and chopped

1. In a large bowl, toss pork ribs with taco seasoning. Cover and refrigerate overnight.
2. Place pork in a slow cooker. In a small bowl, combine the salsa, preServes and barbecue sauce. Pour over ribs. Cover and press the Slow Cook button, and cook on low for 5 to 6 hours or until meat is tender. (Press Slow Cook again to toggle between Low and High cooking temperatures.)
3. Add peaches; cover and cook 30 minutes longer or until peaches are tender.

Indian Tandoori Lamb

Prep time: 20 minutes | **Cook time:** 3 hours | **Serves** 8

- 1½ cups plain yogurt
- 2 tablespoons fresh lemon juice
- 4 cloves garlic, minced
- 1½ teaspoons ground cumin
- 1½ teaspoons garam masala
- 1 teaspoon ground coriander
- Pinch of cayenne pepper
- 1 teaspoon salt
- 3 pounds (1.4 kg) lamb shoulder, fat trimmed and cut into 1-inch chunks
- 4 medium Yukon gold potatoes, cut into quarters
- 3 medium carrots, cut into 1-inch lengths
- ½ cup chicken broth

1. Whisk together the yogurt, lemon juice, garlic, and spices in a large bowl. Add the lamb and toss to coat well with the marinade. Cover and refrigerate for at least 2 hours or overnight.
2. Drain the marinade and add the lamb to the insert of a slow cooker. Add the vegetables and broth and stir to combine. Cover and press the Slow Cook button, and cook on high for 3 hours, until the lamb is tender and the vegetables are cooked through. (Press Slow Cook again to toggle between Low and High cooking temperatures.) Skim off any fat from the top of the sauce.
3. Serve from the cooker set on warm.

Dijon Lemony Leg of Lamb

Prep time: 10 minutes | **Cook time:** 3 to 4 hours | **Serves** 8

- ½ cup Dijon mustard
- ¼ cup fresh lemon juice
- Grated zest of 2 lemons
- 6 garlic cloves, minced
- ¼ cup extra-virgin olive oil
- 1 teaspoon dried oregano
- 1 teaspoon salt
- ½ teaspoon freshly ground black pepper
- 1 (3- to 4-pound / 1.4- to 1.8-kg) boneless leg of lamb, butterflied, fat trimmed
- 1 cup dry white wine
- ½ cup finely chopped fresh Italian parsley

1. Combine the mustard, lemon juice, zest, garlic, oil, oregano, salt, and pepper in a mixing bowl. Pour the marinade into a zipper-top plastic bag, add the lamb to the bag, and turn it to coat. Seal the bag and refrigerate for at least 8 hours or up to 24 hours.
2. Drain the marinade, and roll the meat into a compact cylinder, tying the meat at 1-inch intervals with kitchen string or silicone loops, and put the lamb in insert of a slow cooker. Add the wine. Cover and press the Slow Cook button, and cook on high for 3 hours to 4 hours, until the meat is tender. (Press Slow Cook again to toggle between Low and High cooking temperatures.) Remove the meat from the slow cooker, cover with aluminum foil, and allow to rest for 20 minutes.
3. Strain the sauce through a fine-mesh sieve into a saucepan and remove any fat from the surface. Boil until the sauce is reduced by half. Taste and adjust the seasonings, adding the parsley to the sauce.
4. Cut the meat into ½-inch-thick slices and serve with the sauce on the side.

Leg of Lamb and Cabbage

Prep time: 10 minutes | **Cook time:** 5$\frac{1}{3}$ to 6$\frac{1}{3}$ hours | **Serves** 4 to 6

- ½ teaspoon allspice berries
- ½ teaspoon black peppercorns
- ½ teaspoon whole cloves
- 1 small leg of lamb (about 2 pounds / 907 g), bone-in or boned and tied
- 2 cups hot chicken broth (optional)
- ½ cup dry white wine (optional)
- ¾ teaspoon to 1 teaspoon salt, to your taste
- 1 head cabbage, cored and cut into 8 wedges

1. Put the allspice berries, peppercorns, and cloves in a cheesecloth bag or tea ball and set aside.
2. Put the lamb in the slow cooker. If you are using a round cooker, put the lamb in meaty end down. Add the broth and wine, if using. Add hot water to cover the lamb by an inch. Add the salt, using the lesser amount if you used salted chicken broth. Add the spice ball. Cover and press the Slow Cook button, and cook on high for 1 hour. (Press Slow Cook again to toggle between Low and High cooking temperatures.)
3. Turn the cooker to cook on low for 4 to 5 hours, until the lamb is fork-tender. (Press Slow Cook again to toggle between Low and High cooking temperatures.) About 20 minutes before it is done, preheat the oven to 200ºF (93ºC).
4. Transfer the lamb to a platter, tent with aluminum foil, and place in the oven to keep warm. Put the cabbage wedges in the hot broth remaining in the cooker, cover, and turn the heat to high. Cook until tender, 20 to 30 minutes.
5. Just before cabbage is done, carve the meat. Serve the lamb in shallow bowls with 1 or 2 wedges of cabbage and some of the broth.

CHAPTER 11 FISH AND SEAFOOD

Cheddar Tuna-Stuffed Potatoes

Prep time: 10 minutes | **Cook time:** 3¾ to 6 hours | **Serves** 4

- 4 medium-size Idaho or russet potatoes, scrubbed
- ¾ cup finely shredded Cheddar cheese
- ¼ cup milk
- 1 (6-ounce / 170-g) can water-packed tuna, drained
- ½ cup sour cream
- 1 green onion (white and some of the green), thinly sliced

1. Prick each dripping-wet potato with a fork or the tip of a sharp knife and pile them into the slow cooker; do not add water. Cover and press the Slow Cook button, and cook on low for 6 to 8 hours or on high for 3 to 5 hours, until fork-tender. (Press Slow Cook again to toggle between Low and High cooking temperatures.).
2. Remove the potatoes from the cooker with tongs and cut in half lengthwise. Scoop out the center of each half with a large spoon, leaving enough potato to keep the shell intact. Put the potato flesh in a bowl and add ½ cup of the cheese, the milk, tuna, sour cream, and green onion. Mash the filling with a fork and spoon it back into the shells, mounding it high. Return to the slow cooker, setting down the stuffed potatoes in a single layer if possible so that they touch each other. Sprinkle with the remaining ¼ cup of cheese. Cover and cook on high for 45 minutes to 1 hour. Remove carefully from the cooker and serve immediately.

Sweet and Hot Salmon

Prep time: 5 minutes | **Cook time:** 1½ hours | **Serves** 6

- 3 pounds (1.4 kg) salmon fillets
- ½ cup Colman's English mustard
- ¼ cup honey
- 2 tablespoons finely chopped fresh dill

1. Place the salmon in the insert of a slow cooker. Put the mustard, honey, and dill in a small bowl and stir to combine.
2. Pour the mixture over the salmon, spreading evenly.
3. Cover and press the Slow Cook button, and cook on high for 1½ hours, until the salmon is cooked through. (Press Slow Cook again to toggle between Low and High cooking temperatures.)
4. Serve the salmon from the slow cooker topped with some of the sauce.

Smoky Salmon Fettuccine

Prep time: 10 minutes | **Cook time:** 1 to 2 hours | **Serves** 4

- 2 cups heavy cream
- 3 to 4 ounces (85 to 113 g) top quality lox or smoked salmon, chopped or flaked into ½-inch pieces
- 1 pound (454 g) fresh fettuccine, regular egg or spinach flavored
- 2 tablespoons olive oil (optional)
- Freshly ground black pepper, to taste

1. Combine the cream and the lox in the slow cooker. Cover and press the Slow Cook button, and cook on low for 1 to 2 hours, until very hot. (Press Slow Cook again to toggle between Low and High cooking temperatures.)
2. Meanwhile, cook the fettuccine in boiling water until tender to the bite, about 3 minutes. Take care not to overcook. Toss with the olive oil if the pasta is to stand for over 5 minutes. Add the fettuccine to the hot sauce and toss to coat evenly. If your cooker is large enough, just add the pasta to the cooker; if not, pour the sauce over the pasta in a shallow, heated bowl. Garnish with a few grinds of black pepper and serve immediately.

Cheesy Halibut with Salsa

Prep time: 10 minutes | **Cook time:** 2½ to 2¾ hours | **Serves** 6

- 3 cups prepared medium-hot salsa
- 2 tablespoons fresh lime juice
- 1 teaspoon ground cumin
- 2 to 3 pounds (907 g to 1.4 kg) halibut fillets
- 1½ cup finely shredded Monterey Jack cheese (or Pepper Jack for a spicy topping)

1. Combine the salsa, lime juice, and cumin in the insert of a slow cooker and stir. Cover the slow cooker and press the Slow Cook button, and cook on low for 2 hours. (Press Slow Cook again to toggle between Low and High cooking temperatures.)
2. Put the halibut in the cooker and spoon some of the sauce over the top of the fish. Sprinkle the cheese evenly over the fish. Cover and cook for an additional 30 to 45 minutes.
3. Remove the halibut from the slow cooker and serve on a bed of the sauce.

Miso-Honey Poached Salmon

Prep time: 5 minutes | **Cook time:** 1½ hours | **Serves** 8

- 3 pounds (1.4 kg) salmon fillets
- 3 tablespoons white Miso
- 3 tablespoons honey
- ¼ cup rice wine (mirin) or dry sherry
- 2 teaspoons freshly grated ginger

1. Place the salmon in the insert of a slow cooker.
2. Combine the miso, honey, rice wine, and ginger in a mixing bowl and stir.
3. Pour the sauce over the salmon in the slow cooker. Cover and press the Slow Cook button, and cook on high for 1½ hours, until the salmon is cooked through and registers 165°F (74°C) on an instant-read thermometer inserted in the center of a thick fillet. (Press Slow Cook again to toggle between Low and High cooking temperatures.)
4. Carefully remove the salmon from the slow-cooker insert with a large spatula. Remove the skin from the underside of the salmon (if necessary) and arrange the salmon on a serving platter.
5. Strain the sauce through a fine-mesh sieve into a saucepan. Boil the sauce, reduce it to a syrupy consistency, and serve with the salmon.

Buttery Halibut with Garlic

Prep time: 10 minutes | **Cook time:** 4¾ hours | **Serves** 6

- 1 cup (2 sticks) unsalted butter
- ½ cup olive oil
- 6 cloves garlic, sliced
- 1 teaspoon sweet paprika
- ½ cup lemon juice
- Grated zest of 1 lemon
- ¼ cup finely chopped fresh chives
- 2 to 3 pounds (907 g to 1.4 kg) halibut fillets
- ½ cup finely chopped fresh Italian parsley

1. Combine the butter, oil, garlic, paprika, lemon juice, zest, and chives in the insert of a slow cooker and stir to combine. Cover and press the Slow Cook button, and cook on low for 4 hours. (Press Slow Cook again to toggle between Low and High cooking temperatures.)
2. Add the halibut to the pot, spooning the sauce over the halibut. Cover and cook for an additional 40 minutes, until the halibut is cooked through and opaque.
3. Sprinkle the parsley evenly over the fish and serve immediately.

Lemon-Dijon Orange Roughy

Prep time: 5 minutes | **Cook time:** 3 hours | **Serves** 4

- 1½ pounds (680 g) orange roughy fillets
- 2 tablespoons Dijon mustard
- 3 tablespoons butter, melted
- 1 teaspoon Worcestershire sauce
- 1 tablespoon lemon juice

1. Cut fillets to fit in the slow cooker.
2. In a bowl, mix remaining ingredients together. Pour sauce over fish. (If you have to stack the fish, spoon a portion of the sauce over the first layer of fish before adding the second layer.)
3. Cover and press the Slow Cook button, and cook on low for 3 hours, or until fish flakes easily but is not dry or overcooked. (Press Slow Cook again to toggle between Low and High cooking temperatures.)

Scallops Braised in Dry Sherry

Prep time: 10 minutes | **Cook time:** 4½ hours | **Serves** 6

- 1 cup (2 sticks) unsalted butter
- 2 tablespoons olive oil
- 2 cloves garlic, minced
- 2 teaspoons sweet paprika
- ¼ cup dry sherry
- 2 pounds (907 g) dry-pack sea scallops
- ½ cup finely chopped fresh Italian parsley

1. Put the butter, oil, garlic, paprika, and sherry in the insert of a slower cooker.
2. Cover and press the Slow Cook button, and cook on low for 4 hours. (Press Slow Cook again to toggle between Low and High cooking temperatures.) Add the scallops, tossing them in the butter sauce. Cover and press the Slow Cook button, and cook on high for 30 to 40 minutes, until the scallops are opaque. (Press Slow Cook again to toggle between Low and High cooking temperatures.)
3. Transfer the scallops and sauce from the slow cooker to a serving platter. Sprinkle with the parsley and serve.

Cheesy Salmon Casserole

Prep time: 10 minutes | **Cook time:** 2½ to 3½ hours | **Serves** 6

- 1 (14¾-ounce / 418-g) can salmon with liquid
- 1 (4-ounce / 113-g) can mushrooms, drained
- 1½ cups bread crumbs
- ⅓ cup eggbeaters
- 1 cup shredded fat-free cheese
- 1 tablespoon lemon juice
- 1 tablespoon minced onion

1. Flake fish in a bowl, removing bones. Stir in remaining ingredients. Pour into lightly greased slow cooker.
2. Cover. Press the Slow Cook button, and cook on low for 2½ to 3½ hours. (Press Slow Cook again to toggle between Low and High cooking temperatures.)

Tuna and Egg Casserole

Prep time: 10 minutes | **Cook time:** 5 to 8 hours | **Serves** 4

- 2 (7-ounce / 198-g) cans tuna
- 1 (10¾-ounce / 305-g) can cream of celery soup
- 3 hard-boiled eggs, chopped
- ½ to 1½ cups diced celery
- ½ cup diced onions
- ½ cup mayonnaise
- ¼ teaspoon ground pepper
- 1½ cups crushed potato chips

1. Combine all ingredients except ¼ cup potato chips in slow cooker. Top with remaining chips.
2. Cover. Press the Slow Cook button, and cook on low for 5 to 8 hours. (Press Slow Cook again to toggle between Low and High cooking temperatures.)

Garlicky Crab in White Wine

Prep time: 10 minutes | **Cook time:** 5½ hours | **Serves** 6 to 8

- 1 cup (2 sticks) unsalted butter
- ½ cup olive oil
- 10 cloves garlic, sliced
- 2 tablespoons Old Bay seasoning
- 2 cups dry white wine or vermouth
- 1 lemon, thinly sliced
- 3 to 4 pounds (1.4 to 1.8 kg) cooked crab legs and claws, cracked

1. Put the butter, oil, garlic, seasoning, wine, and lemon in the insert of a slow cooker.
2. Cover and press the Slow Cook button, and cook on low for 4 hours. (Press Slow Cook again to toggle between Low and High cooking temperatures.) Add the crab, spoon the sauce over the crab, and cook for an additional 1½ hours, turning the crab in the sauce during cooking.
3. Serve the crab from the cooker set on warm.

Creamy Shrimp Curry

Prep time: 5 minutes | **Cook time:** 2 to 3 hours | **Serves** 4 to 5

- 1 small onion, chopped
- 2 cups cooked shrimp
- 1 teaspoon curry powder
- 1 (10¾-ounce / 305-g) can cream of mushroom soup
- 1 cup sour cream

1. Combine all ingredients except sour cream in a slow cooker.
2. Cover. Press the Slow Cook button, and cook on low for 2 to 3 hours. (Press Slow Cook again to toggle between Low and High cooking temperatures.)
3. Ten minutes before serving, stir in sour cream.
4. Serve over rice or puff pastry.

CHAPTER 12

RICE, GRAINS, AND BEANS

Converted White Rice

Prep time: 5 minutes | **Cook time:** 1½ hours | **Serves** 4

- 1 cup converted white rice
- 2 cups water
- ½ teaspoon salt (optional)
- 1 tablespoon unsalted butter (optional)

1. Place the rice, water, and salt (if using) in the slow cooker and stir to combine. Use a spoon to smooth the rice into as even a layer as possible. Add the butter, if using. Cover and press the Slow Cook button, and cook on low for 2½ hours or on high for 1½ hours. (Press Slow Cook again to toggle between Low and High cooking temperatures.)
2. Turn off the cooker. Use a fork to gently stir and fluff the rice, breaking up any clumps. Serve immediately. Or, if you are not ready to eat, cover the rice. It will stay hot for about 1 hour. (Leave the insert in the cooker to help conserve the heat.)

Braised Chickpeas with Cilantro

Prep time: 10 minutes | **Cook time:** 8 to 9 hours | **Serves** 6

- 1 red onion, halved and thinly sliced
- 1 tablespoon extra-virgin olive oil
- 1 tablespoon smoked paprika
- Salt and pepper, to taste
- 3 cups vegetable or chicken broth, plus extra as needed
- 3 cups water
- 1 pound (454 g) dried chickpeas, picked over and rinsed
- ¼ cup minced fresh cilantro

1. Microwave onion, oil, paprika, and 1 teaspoon salt in bowl, stirring occasionally, until onion is softened, about 5 minutes. Transfer to a slow cooker. Stir in broth, water, and chickpeas. Cover and press the Slow Cook button, and cook on high for 8 to 9 hours, until chickpeas are tender. (Press Slow Cook again to toggle between Low and High cooking temperatures.)
2. Drain chickpeas, reserving 1 cup cooking liquid. Return one-third of chickpeas and reserved cooking liquid to the slow cooker and mash with potato masher until smooth. Stir in remaining chickpeas and cilantro. Season with salt and pepper to taste. Serve. (Chickpeas can be held on warm or low setting for up to 2 hours; adjust consistency with extra hot broth as needed before serving.)

Creamy Saffron Rice

Prep time: 10 minutes | **Cook time:** 1½ to 2 hours | **Serves** 6

- 1⅓ cups basmati rice
- Pinch saffron
- 1 tablespoon vegetable oil
- 1 teaspoon cumin seeds
- 3⅓ cups hot water
- 1 teaspoon salt
- 1 tablespoon butter
- 4 tablespoons cream

1. Wash the rice in two or three changes of water until the water runs clear. Then leave it to soak in warm water while you prep the rest of the dish.
2. Grind a few threads of saffron in a mortar and pestle. Add 2 tablespoons of hot water and stir. Set aside.
3. Preheat the slow cooker to high and add the oil. Add the cumin seeds and let them toast.
4. Pour the hot water, salt, butter, and cream into the slow cooker. Strain the soaked rice and add to the slow cooker.
5. Stir and cover with the lid. Press the Slow Cook button, and cook on high for 1½ to 2 hours. (Press Slow Cook again to toggle between Low and High cooking temperatures.) Halfway through the cooking, very gently stir the rice.
6. Turn off the cooker and sprinkle in the saffron water. Let it stand, uncovered, for 5 to 10 minutes. Fluff the rice with a fork and serve.

Orange Pearl Barley with Apple

Prep time: 10 minutes | **Cook time:** 3 to 4 hours | **Serves** 4

- 1 cup orange juice
- 1 cup vegetable or chicken broth
- ⅓ cup pearl barley
- ¼ cup dried currants
- ¼ cup dried apricots, cut into strips
- ¼ cup chopped pitted dates
- 1 tart apple, peeled, cored, and chopped
- 2 tablespoons chopped pecans

1. Combine all the ingredients in the slow cooker and stir to distribute them evenly.
2. Cover and press the Slow Cook button, and cook on low for 3 to 4 hours. (Press Slow Cook again to toggle between Low and High cooking temperatures.) Serve hot.

Almond-Mushroom Wild Rice

Prep time: 10 minutes | **Cook time:** 4½ to 6 hours | **Serves** 6

- 2 cups wild rice
- 1 cup slivered almonds
- 1 to 2 shallots, finely chopped
- ½ cup finely chopped celery
- 8 ounces (227 g) fresh mushrooms, chopped or sliced
- 6 cups vegetable broth
- Salt and freshly ground black pepper, to taste

1. Rinse the rice under cold running water until the water runs clear, then drain.
2. Place all the ingredients except the salt and pepper in the slow cooker. Stir to combine. Cover and press the Slow Cook button, and cook on low for 4½ to 6 hours, until the kernels are open and tender. (Press Slow Cook again to toggle between Low and High cooking temperatures.) Do not remove the lid before the rice has cooked at least 4 hours.
3. Season with salt and pepper, and serve immediately.

Red Kidney Bean Curry

Prep time: 15 minutes | **Cook time:** 8 hours | **Serves** 6

- 1½ cups red kidney beans
- 4 cups hot water
- 7 to 8 ounces (198 to 227 g) canned plum tomatoes
- 2 teaspoons freshly grated ginger
- 1 teaspoon salt, plus more for seasoning
- 1 teaspoon turmeric
- 4 garlic cloves, finely chopped
- 1 or 2 fresh green chiles, sliced
- 1 onion, finely diced
- 1 teaspoon garam masala
- Handful fresh coriander leaves, chopped
- 1 teaspoon butter (optional)

1. Soak the kidney beans overnight, then rinse. If you have a boil function on your slow cooker, cover the beans with water and boil for 10 minutes. If not, do this in a large pot. Drain and put the beans back into the slow cooker.
2. Add the remaining ingredients except the garam masala, coriander leaves, and butter. Cover and press the Slow Cook button, and cook on low for 8 hours, or on high for 6 hours. (Press Slow Cook again to toggle between Low and High cooking temperatures.)
3. Add the garam masala, chopped coriander leaves, and butter (if using). Season with salt and serve.

Parmesan Polenta

Prep time: 5 minutes | **Cook time:** 6 hours | **Serves** 8

- 7½ cups water
- 1½ cups coarse-ground yellow polenta
- 1½ teaspoons salt
- ½ cup (1 stick) unsalted butter
- 1 cup grated or shredded Parmesan or Italian fontina cheese

1. Whisk the water, polenta, and salt together in the slow cooker for a few seconds. Cover and press the Slow Cook button, and cook on high for 30 minutes to 1 hour to heat the water. (Press Slow Cook again to toggle between Low and High cooking temperatures.)
2. Stir with a wooden spoon, cover, turn the cooker to cook on low for about 5 hours, stirring occasionally. The polenta will thicken quite quickly after 2 hours, sort of expand magically in the cooker, and look done, but it will need the extra time to cook all the grains evenly. At 5 hours, taste and make sure the desired consistency has been reached and all the grains are tender. The longer the polenta cooks, the creamier it will become. When done, it will be smooth, very thick (yet pourable), and a wooden spoon will stand up by itself without falling over (the true test). The polenta will be fine on low for an additional hour, if necessary. Add a bit more hot water if it gets too stiff.
3. To serve as a mound of soft polenta, portion out with an oversized spoon onto plates or into shallow soup bowls. Top each serving with a pat of the butter and sprinkle with some of the cheese. Serve immediately.

Tuscan-Style White Beans with Herbs

Prep time: 10 minutes | **Cook time:** 2½ to 3½ hours | **Serves** 6

- 2½ cups dried white beans, such as great northern or navy
- 2 sprigs fresh sage
- 1 bay leaf
- 1 head garlic, left whole and unpeeled
- 10 cups water
- 1 tablespoon coarse sea salt, or more to taste
- A few grinds of black pepper
- Extra-virgin olive oil, for serving

1. Put the beans in a colander and rinse under cold running water, picking over for damaged beans and small stones. Transfer to the slow cooker and cover by 3 inches with cold water. Soak for 6 to 12 hours and then drain.

2. Add the sage, bay leaf, garlic, and 10 cups of water. Cover and press the Slow Cook button, and cook on high for 2½ to 3½ hours. (Press Slow Cook again to toggle between Low and High cooking temperatures.) The beans need to be covered with liquid at all times to cook properly. When done, they will be tender and hold their shape, rather than fall apart. Toward the end of the cooking time, add the sea salt and remove the bay leaf and head of garlic (you can squeeze the cooked garlic back into the beans if you like or discard).
3. Let the beans cool in the cooker for 1 hour, uncovered, then drain off all but ½ cup of the liquid. Serve, seasoned with more salt and several grinds of black pepper, and drizzled with olive oil.

Garlicky White Beans with Sage

Prep time: 10 minutes | **Cook time:** 8 to 9 hours | **Serves** 6

- 1 onion, finely chopped
- 5 garlic cloves, minced
- 3 tablespoons extra-virgin olive oil, divided
- 2 teaspoons minced fresh sage, divided
- Salt and pepper, to taste
- 3 cups vegetable or chicken broth, plus extra as needed
- 3 cups water
- 1 pound (454 g) dried small white beans, picked over and rinsed

1. Microwave onion, garlic, 1 tablespoon oil, 1 teaspoon sage, and 1 teaspoon salt in a bowl, stirring occasionally, until onion is softened, about 5 minutes. Transfer to a slow cooker. Stir in broth, water, and beans. Cover and press the Slow Cook button, and cook on high for 8 to 9 hours, until beans are tender. (Press Slow Cook again to toggle between Low and High cooking temperatures.)
2. Drain beans, reserving 1 cup cooking liquid. Return one-third of beans and reserved cooking liquid to the slow cooker and mash with potato masher until smooth. Stir in remaining beans, remaining 2 tablespoons oil, and remaining 1 teaspoon sage. Season with salt and pepper to taste. Serve. (Beans can be held on warm or low setting for up to 2 hours; adjust consistency with extra hot broth as needed before serving.)

Appendix 1: Measurement Conversion Chart

VOLUME EQUIVALENTS(DRY)

US STANDARD	METRIC (APPROXIMATE)
1/8 teaspoon	0.5 mL
1/4 teaspoon	1 mL
1/2 teaspoon	2 mL
3/4 teaspoon	4 mL
1 teaspoon	5 mL
1 tablespoon	15 mL
1/4 cup	59 mL
1/2 cup	118 mL
3/4 cup	177 mL
1 cup	235 mL
2 cups	475 mL
3 cups	700 mL
4 cups	1 L

WEIGHT EQUIVALENTS

US STANDARD	METRIC (APPROXIMATE)
1 ounce	28 g
2 ounces	57 g
5 ounces	142 g
10 ounces	284 g
15 ounces	425 g
16 ounces (1 pound)	455 g
1.5 pounds	680 g
2 pounds	907 g

VOLUME EQUIVALENTS(LIQUID)

US STANDARD	US STANDARD (OUNCES)	METRIC (APPROXIMATE)
2 tablespoons	1 fl.oz.	30 mL
1/4 cup	2 fl.oz.	60 mL
1/2 cup	4 fl.oz.	120 mL
1 cup	8 fl.oz.	240 mL
1 1/2 cup	12 fl.oz.	355 mL
2 cups or 1 pint	16 fl.oz.	475 mL
4 cups or 1 quart	32 fl.oz.	1 L
1 gallon	128 fl.oz.	4 L

TEMPERATURES EQUIVALENTS

FAHRENHEIT(F)	CELSIUS(C) (APPROXIMATE)
225 °F	107 °C
250 °F	120 °C
275 °F	135 °C
300 °F	150 °C
325 °F	160 °C
350 °F	180 °C
375 °F	190 °C
400 °F	205 °C
425 °F	220 °C
450 °F	235 °C
475 °F	245 °C
500 °F	260 °C

Appendix 2: Recipe Index

CPSIA information can be obtained
at www.ICGtesting.com
Printed in the USA
LVHW060755260121
677404LV00006B/301

9 781637 33167